The Risen Lady

—DEVOTIONAL—

ROYALTY BOOKS

The Risen Lady Devotional

First Edition

First published by Royalty Books,
Harare, 2022

Copyright © contributors 2022

All rights reserved. No part of this publication may be reproduced, stored in a retrieval system, or transmitted in any form or by any means mechanical or electronic, photocopying or otherwise, without the prior permission of the authors.

Edited by Phillip Kundeni Chidavaenzi

Text set in Aldine 721 by Royalty Books

CONTENTS

Risen Ladies	*i*
Dedication	*v*
Acknowledgments	*vii*
Foreword	*ix*
The Breaking of a Teenager's Heart	*1*
Before I Became	*13*
Focus on the Journey	*26*
Prayer: Master Key that Unlocks Doors	*37*
Navigating Unchartered Territories	*44*
Grace and Mercy Abound	*77*
From Trauma to Transformation	*89*
Righteousness by Faith	*108*

RISEN LADIES

Angeline Nyabepu

United Kingdom-based minister of the gospel, Angeline Nyabepu, is the founder of Loveflow Ministries. She is a life coach, mentor and counsellor at Prosper My Soul. A prophetic worshipper, Angeline sings songs of healing, freedom and deliverance. She graduated from Charis Bible College and holds a BA Honours in Theology from Newman University. She has published a motivational book titled *Whispers of Encouragement*.

Laurencia Solomon

Laurencia Solomon is a mother of three and a full-time career woman, she has been a banker for about 9 years. She holds a Diploma in Business Administration, Degree in Business Management & HR both from (Wolverhampton University) and Master of Laws from (OU). A founder of ALL Community Network Projects, a charity that seeks to make a big impact in the lives of others in the smallest possible ways and inspire to aspire through giving and demonstrating how, "it does not take riches to reach out". In 2018, the charity successfully organised a youth conference in England that gave the youth the opportunity to discover themselves through the mentoring from local role models. Laurencia was born in England but grew up in Ghana and returned to England age 19, she currently lives in England with her family. She enjoys worshipping God through singing and preaching. Laurencia loves travelling, baking and event decorating, her love for baking has now turned into a small business.

Adesuwa Omoregie Ogie

Adesuwa Omoregie Ogie is the founder of Essence Oasis Family Outreach. An ambassador of Christ, she is a mother, wife, author, family advocate and inspirational encourager.

Chiedza Nyakuwa

Chiedza Nyakuwa lives in Chitungwiza, Zimbabwe with her husband and two children. She works for Knight Frank as a Personal Assistant. She believes in the power of prayer. She is a woman of faith who wants to see people in her sphere of influence prosper. She loves coming along people who have had long unsolved issues and offer her services as an intercessor. Chiedza also serves in her local church and is part of Loveflow Ministries Global leadership. She is passionate about cooking, baking, visiting recreational facilities and reading the Bible with her family.

Pao Viola Mbewe

Pao Viola Mbewe Born of Benson Vasco Jim (RIP) and Bessie Flossie Jedegwa in 1967, Pao is the youngest of ten — amid the loss of six siblings who, below age fifty, passed on to glory. An engaging author focusing on God's power in turbulent times, she imparts wisdom derived from the poignancy of her lived experiences, to rise after every fall – above the storms of life. Her endeavour to SOAR as an eagle, displays a heavy dependence on God as the wind beneath her wings by trusting Him unreservedly, even through waiting seasons — that Pao describes as the Hallway. Born, bred, and educated in Blantyre, Malawi, Pao wed her university sweetheart in 1991 and immediately relocated to Botswana and, later in 2005, the United Kingdom. Of Adventist origin, her life features an authentic faith in reverence surrender to God, serving in Methodist and the Pentecostal ministries in Southern Africa and UK. Embodying selfless attributes, Pao engages to encourage, equip, and empower others — achieving wholeness and contentment with an Agape love of Christ. Her passion for Holistic wellbeing and service in the NHS, Hospice and Charities settings... set her apart to impact her world. A professional as a Chartered Accountant, Pao holds a B.Com in BA & Marketing, an MA in Leadership and Management. She upholds holistic life values in the paradigms of Reengineering Business Systems and Services, Engaging Emotional Intelligence and Reframing Mindsets, to triumph in life. Volunteering in communities — her services extend to Prison service under the Ministry of Justice in UK and the equivalent settings in Malawi.

Nunudzai S. T Ngorora

Nunudzai S.T. Ngorora was born in Bonda, Nyanga in Zimbabwe's Manicaland Province. She is a widowed mother of four boys. She currently lives in Zimbabwe with her two younger sons. She is a counsellor, teacher, trainer, translator, and Interpreter of modern languages. Nunudzai describes herself as eclectic, an agent of change, a catalyst, a voice for the voiceless. She is a social entrepreneur-cum-communicator and passionate about transformative authentic leadership.

Glad Bartram

Glad Bartram is a life coach, mentor and positive mindset therapist. She helps people struggling with depression and trauma from domestic abuse. Although she is originally from Zimbabwe, she lives with her daughter in England.

Stella Murove

Stella Murove is a mother and grandmother who is married to Suprine Murove, the pastor of Life Christian Centre in Beechdale, Walsall. In 2015, Stella graduated from Charis Bible College, where she spent three years studying the Bible and was also awarded a Certificate in Leadership by Open University. Stella holds a post-graduate certificate in Education by Wolverhampton University and has been teaching Mathematics and Science in secondary schools in the United Kingdom for six years. Prior to that, Stella taught in Zimbabwe, where she was born and spent the first 11 years of her life. From a tender age Stella has always been passionate about teaching. She enjoys teaching the word of God and this is her calling.

DEDICATION

RISEN Lady, you are powerful, and strong. You are a phoenix, an eagle that rises in the storm and I want to congratulate you for being a pioneer in "The Risen Lady" Series. The journey hasn't been easy, but you showed determination and courage in sharing your experiences with us. I am reminded of a precious woman who arose during a very difficult situation, which seemed as if it would never change, her husband reassured her that he was happy with her, and she should be content with that. Hannah was mocked by Peninnah, her husband's wife, who seemed to have everything Hannah wanted, tormented, ridiculed, put to shame, and had no voice. However, in her tenacity, anguish of soul and trust in the One who created her, she stood and saw her victory come to pass. Hannah did not settle for what everyone thought was enough for her; she knew what was for her and she got hold of it, once identified with bareness she overcame and held a child who became a man of honour and distinction (1 Samuel 1:2-2:21). To all those Risen Ladies like Hannah, who have shown us the way we dedicate this pioneer book to you.

Women are resilient; we struggle with a lot of internal and external problems and yet every day we show up and multitask as if everything is perfect. It is time for us to realise that we are a special gift to our communities, children, spouses and even to ourselves. We are awesome and we can celebrate ourselves every day without apology. It's time to accept who you are glittering special jewel. You are not complex but intelligently designed for the purpose of your existence. Though we may be unique, we have so many similarities in that we are created to give life. Not only in carrying children but life in the environments that we exist, we carry a strength that cannot be measured, oppressed, or limited by life's challenges.

I dedicate this book to The Risen lady who has contributed her story, invited us in a small section of her life, and showed us how to stand and fight for her freedom by allowing Christ to be the centre of it. Moreover, I want to dedicate it to Risen Ladies Ministries, who continue to rise, encourage, and motivate others to keep shining, work in their callings and pray for other women. In addition, I dedicate this book to the unknown Risen lady who has risen from a life of slumber, has now embraced her path and who she is in life. Furthermore, to the one who is still wondering if they will rise, if they will be counted as a Risen Lady, I say yes, you will rise! Lastly, I dedicate it to my mother, a strong Risen Lady who has always empowered me to rise above every storm that came my way.

ACKNOWLEDGEMENTS

WITHOUT God, nothing can be done (John 15:5). Everything belongs to Him (Psalms 24) He is the One who gives ideas, strength, and encouragement. I would like to acknowledge God, for His great love, great grace. In every project I do The Holy Spirit is my great consultant, counsellor, advisor, and motivator. I have become to depend on Him for every move, His voice is the most valued thing in my life, and I thank Him for the honour of trusting me with His precious work. I acknowledge Tonderai, my beautiful son, for continually understanding and going along with my very busy lifestyle, especially with all the endless work I embark on, a true gift from God.

I would want to acknowledge my parents, Mr. and Mrs. Nyabepu, together with my siblings who are a constant source of support in everything I do. To Tanya Chitunhu, a friend who believes in what God has bestowed in me, you are awesome. I acknowledge the amazing Risen Ladies who have contributed to Volume 1, Laurencia R. Solomon, Adesuwa Omeregie Ogie, Chiedza Nyakuwa, Pao Viola Mbewe, Nunudzai S.T Ngorora, Glad Bartram and Stella Murove. You are exceptional ladies and pioneers of great things to come. Thank you for your tenacity and participation in this ground-breaking project.

I acknowledge, Loveflow Ministries Global for faithfulness in serving God with me and praying behind the scenes. May God continue to bless you and raise you up to places you never imagined or dreamt of. Enjoy *The Risen Lady*

Let the Loveflow x
Angeline

FOREWORD

Dear Reader

A new day, a new dawn...

The sun rises and illuminates the day with light; the dark stormy, turbulent night has passed.

As darkness passes, we observe the beautiful, bright sunlight, and we see clearly and realise that the dark phases of our lives are not permanent. The darkness of ignorance, abuse, heartbreak and betrayal, illness, and disease, broken promises and bereavement is temporary. We discover that light comes with knowledge, soul searching, "becoming," discovering purpose and our calling. The Psalmist reminds us, "Weeping may endure for a night, but joy cometh in the morning." (**Psalms 30:5**).

Angeline Nyabepu brings together women from different walks of life. Women who read the stories of others in the time past. Women who have risen, taken a stand, and decided to tell their stories in their own voices. Their voice of experience, breaking barriers, overcoming, and empowering self and others.

The Risen Lady takes you on a journey; step by step as if handheld, "she" will guide you through a time of questioning, self-doubt, trials, and challenges. The rawness of the truth in the storytelling makes it relatable and inspires you to shake of the dust and rise. Isaiah exhorts, "Shake yourself from the dust; arise, sit [on your throne], Jerusalem: release yourself from the bonds of your neck, captive daughter of Zion." (**Isaiah 52:2**).

Chapter by chapter, we see her rising; "the woman," not silenced anymore, not restrained, breaking boundaries and, against all odds, making it through. She pursues knowledge, education, forgiveness, and love; the love of self, and self-belief. She rises beyond setbacks and navigates her way through accusations, rejection, loss, bereavement, including financial difficulties. Her story is the story of many; only she has risen and decided to speak up with her pen. She is "the risen lady".

Her rising is anchored by the living word of God. No matter where she is, whatever she is going through, she rises, propelled by her faith.

I met Angeline in my line of work where I empower women on Dear Auntiey Mimiey. Angeline is a Christian minister and coach. She is passionate about her faith. She is consistent, committed and does not compromise on her calling. She rose to obedience and thrives when others thrive. She is the testament of a risen lady and very much qualified to spearhead "the Risen lady project!" that is birthed in this book by risen lady authors.

Be blessed and empowered!

Mirriam Kwenda Mutize
(Dear Auntiey Mimiey)

1

The Breaking of a Teenager's Heart

ANGELINE NYABEPU

IT was on a Monday morning and we had just finished getting ready for the school day. I was in Form 3 at a church-run boarding school in Centenary, Zimbabwe. We did not have the privilege of a school caretaker or cleaner so we, the students, had to do the chores ourselves. We understood the dynamics of the school system. Although there was academic education, we were also taught on how important it was to also use our hands. The duties we carried out included cleaning our toilets, the piggery, feeding the chickens and sorting out the insides of a cow after slaughter.

I used to share a dormitory with seven other girls. We took turns to clean up the shower and toilet rooms. This Monday was our dorm's turn. I remember going to clean after everyone had finished bathing. However, while I was cleaning up, I saw a girl come in with the matron. The matron asked me to stretch out my hand so that she could give me some beatings in my palm. There was no room for questions or explanation for what was happening. Schools in Zimbabwe believed in the dictum, spare the rod spoils the child. It was normal for a teacher or matron to punish a student by the stick.

In this particular case, however, I was not notified why I was getting punished. Nevertheless, I let my hand out in obedience and received the beating. I took the beating without flinching because I had developed a coping mechanism of feeling the pain once and dealing with it later. Looking back, I do not think the matron liked the fact that I did not flinch and probably felt it was a challenge to her.

She instructed me to go with her to the deputy headmaster's office. I still did not have a clue why all this was happening. Most of the other girls in the other dormitories had come out to witness what was happening. I went into a state of confusion, but I just followed the matron's instructions. It was a walk of shame as we headed to the deputy headmaster's office, ignoring the stares and comments from the other girls that had gathered to witness the drama. As we passed through the classroom blocks, the boys also witnessed the show as the matron led the way while I followed like a sheep led to the slaughter. As if this scenario was not enough, I had a boyfriend at school and it just made the situation worse. There was no justification; it was just assumed I had messed up big time. Strangely, it seemed everyone else, except me, knew what I had done. I hoped I would know the reason once we got to the deputy headmaster's office. I was told to wait outside. I am giving a summary of this event so that the reader understands how wounds can form from a young age and have far-reaching impact in adult life. This incident laid the foundation of a dysfunctional adult life. The headmaster did not care to ask me about the accusations. That was when I realised there was a lot more happening, though I was in the dark concerning the details of my 'crime'.

The deputy headmaster instructed me to go home and bring my parents. I had to take a two-hour bus drive still wondering about my 'crime'. I had a lot of questions but no answer. I was still trying to process the embarrassment I had gone through that morning and now I had to go home and face my parents. My parents were very strict and did not tolerate any form of delinquency by their children at school. I was numb, frightened and confused. I needed someone to ask me how I felt, but there was no one. I hoped to get solace, comfort, and assurance when I got home. I comforted myself with the hope of getting home and experiencing parental love.

Now my parents were young, and I was their first child. Raising a teenager at that time was also learning ground for them. I arrived home and was summoned to my parents' bedroom, where they asked me what had happened. I did not have an answer for them because I was also still in the dark. My parents took me back to school after a few days. What happened after the visit to school defined how I would act and behave in future? At 15, my life was shattered. I wondered if that was how life was meant to be like.

Once again, I was not allowed to go into the office but I was instructed to stay in the car. My parents and the deputy headmaster had a meeting in my absence. I did not hear what was discussed but the next thing I saw was them come to the car in anger and take my bags out and throw them onto the ground. They got into the car and drove away. I wished they could speak with me, at least ask me, and give me a chance to answer but nothing of that sort happened.

I picked my bags with shame and walked that long walk to the dormitories. I had come from home with cooked chicken, some tuck (food) and money. In my disoriented self I had put the money under my pillow and food in my locker and went to class. Upon arriving back to the room, I saw a bully over my food tucking at my chicken and the money under my pillow had disappeared. I did not have the energy to ask or fight anyone, so I just shut down and kept quiet.

As if the events were not enough, the next morning I was called to the office and given more punishment. I had become numb. I had no power to protest, to argue or ask anything. I just went into a state of shock and did whatever was demanded. The punishment really knocked me down; I was to cut the grass near the boys' dormitory with a slasher then dig a hole the size of my height. I am a tall woman, almost 6 feet, and I had never done this type of work before. It was torturous. As I began to carry out the punishment, the boys would pass by and ask what I had done to go through such punishment but all I could say was that I did not know. Their concern and compassion were the first I received all week and I valued those questions. It gave me a chance to be human because the events of the past days had left me feeling lost and deeply sad. If only someone had notified me of the reason for my punishment, then I would have some closure. However, that did not happen and as I write this today, I have no details concerning what exactly transpired 24 years ago. It's only been six years since I received healing and closure concerning the incident.

Development of the Wound

The incident may seem simple and insignificant, but it became the foundation of a dysfunctional future. My soul developed a wound that no human could heal. No one even knew it was there and no one wanted to know. I learnt to cope with the pain that came from it. There are some things that happened in this scenario that could only be corrected by the divine Spirit of God.

Some girls from my dormitory had snitched on me. They did not tell me what the accusation was. I did not quite know who had got me into trouble, so I put my guard up and did not trust anyone from that moment on in my life. I always had to watch my back and be careful with everything I did. I felt betrayed by those that were meant to be my friends, those girls I shared life with. I was heartbroken, but I had to be strong and not breakdown in front of them. That would have made me seem weak. I had to defend myself as if I had dealt with everything but inside, I was dying, I was crying, I was sad, it hurt but no one was willing to heal. The best thing to do was to push it away in my mind and continue with school as if everything had normalised. However, school was not normal anymore. It became a chore. I was in a constant state of confusion. My grades went down. I had changed. The incident had changed me but only I noticed but did not know what to do.

The matron was supposed to care for me. She was my guardian at school. She was to look after my welfare, but she had betrayed my trust. My opinion of her had been distorted and marred. I could not go to her for anything. My young heart started to realise that it was vulnerable and had no protection. No one cared for its interests or valued its health. Therefore, it started to protect itself in so many ways which were not healthy.

My young parents, who loved me very much in the best way they knew how, probably did what they thought was right at that moment. Though it was right in their eyes, it was not entirely right for everyone. They failed to see the pain that rested in their timid, quiet, hurt, and lonely child. I needed them to defend me, to protect me, to tell me everything was going to be alright, that it would pass. But, instead, in my eyes I felt they closed ranks with the enemy against me. I was left with no one, I was alone, even my own mother and father had abandoned me. There was no one to look after me. Little did I know that there was one who never leaves no forsake us. All this time God knew and cared.

According to African tradition, a child must be silent when adults speak or make decisions. My parents valued the words of the deputy headmaster. It was like whatever the school authorities said was right. They felt that if a child can be told to go and call their parents, then they must have committed a grievous sin. It was a cultural thing. However, it does not really work for the vulnerable young person. Young people have a voice and they have feelings and emotions. If they are not cultivated with care, then a lot of distortions happen around the heart and soul resulting in us seeing behaviours that will just be a cry for help. Young people should be allowed to express themselves in a healthy environment. My relationship with my parents was no longer the same. From that day, I looked at them from a distorted perspective. I had to adjust to their type of love because the one I needed was not available. They had tough love. Sending me to boarding school was their expression of love for me. They wanted me to have a good education, they fed me, and did everything that needed to be done, but they did not know me.

That day they lost a child in my heart. I could not trust that they could protect me. I could not open to them about anything because this is what my heart had registered. I believe that as parents we need to know our children more than anyone does and allow them to express themselves.

Knowing your child can help separate lies and truth that an outsider will tell you. We have to see beyond our children's attitudes and behaviours. There is need to see the person. As parents, we are advocates to our children, we give them a voice. Whatever the case a child might be involved in, we need to discipline within context and care, leaving the child with a lesson learnt as well as healthy emotions. Without a healthy outcome there could be a different number of things that can happen in a child's life. My relationship with my parents stayed the same on the surface but in my heart, I had placed them on a different place, they no longer had a pure innocent child. My personality changed, I became afraid, and I started to hide. I no longer defended myself.

It Matters to God

The things that happen to us in our past can shape our thinking and perspective. The way a child sees the people around and events that happen around them can define the way their future world can be. The incident that happened when I was 15 years old became the basis or motherboard of how I processed life. I developed coping mechanisms for my then present situation which then spiralled into my adult life. They created a dysfunctional life.

As a teenager I learnt to zone out, to be absent in a present moment. Since my heart had no one to protect, it learnt different skills to protect itself. If I did not want to hear the negative words being spoken around me or at me, I would shift in my mind and go to a different place and one would think I was still listening to them. I began to create my own world in my thoughts and my own comforting fantasies that took me away form an environment of pain. Though I used to experience a lot of emotional pain stemming from the event, I learnt to accept pain and would just tell myself that it would pass and go but the truth is it did not go. It got buried inside me and started to work in different ways. I always stayed in the shadows. I was present in the natural but everything about me was hiding. I would not take things near my heart but glazed through things. My heart felt abandoned, orphaned, and neglected, which resulted in me looking for love in wrong places. The Bible says in *3 John 2*, *"Beloved, I pray that you may prosper in all things and be in health, just as your soul prospers."* When one's soul is not healthy and prosperous, nothing in that person's natural life really works. I lived life with a view that I had been given by the incident that happened in my past. I was filled with anger, shame, bitterness, abandonment, and rejection. All these negative emotions rested on that wound that had been created when I was a child. I had become an adult, but my emotions were still in that place of the hurt.

We need to understand that though we may experience growth in the natural if we remain with hurt and baggage from the past, we remain in that place we got hurt. I found myself being successful in other areas but not so in many. I would have a few steps forward and more back; it had become a cycle. However, I had forgotten the reason for these problems.

I began to assume there was witchcraft happening to me. I would bind, loose and curse which would only work for a moment but then again experience the issues. What was happening was that the root of all these causes was not being addressed. I had forgotten that the event in the past had created a wound, which would fester and exhibit itself in so many ways. The only time I remembered about it was when I was hurting, and the pain was connected to the incident.

Forgiveness My Door to Healing

Everything that happens to us matters to God. It was Easter time in 2014 when I had planned to go away for the Easter break. I was about to leave the house and felt that there was an invisible blockage on my door. It dawned on me that I was not to leave the house. I do have a great relationship with the Holy Spirit, and I sensed He wanted to have some time with me. Today I celebrate my obedience on that particular day. It was my day of deliverance and healing. Even those things I had hidden in my heart years ago and those that happened in my adult life, enlarging the wound, mattered to God. He began to show me that I was not alone after all. He watched me all the time and protected me from the intentions of the enemy. The enemy had planned for my downfall and destruction, and wanted to take me for his kingdom at a very young age. God had marked me and chosen me; He was not going to allow evil to prevail over me.

During that Easter week, the Holy Spirt began to share with me the reasons my life was in turmoil. He showed me the number of times I had developed wounds when things had happened and asked me to write all the incidents and people that had hurt me. I did not need to think hard about them. He brought them up for me and began to teach me how to effectively forgive, let go and receive inner wholeness. We focused on everything that had accumulated over the years and when He felt I was ready to deal with the main wound He reminded me of that incident that had happened when I was 15. I did not want to go into that place as I had dismissed it and packed it away. The Lord had to minister to me that if I did not visit my memory to address the issue, then I may be crippled for life and fail to experience wholeness and I would not enjoy the life that He had set before me. It took days for me to come to the point I could open that door in my soul where I had hidden this issue.

I knew that this was going to be a great deliverance because every time I tried to open that door, there was unbearable pain. However, I was ready. I wanted freedom. I began to forgive the way the Lord had taught me and instantly I was back in that place when I was 15. I felt a very excruciating pain in my stomach that diminished as I let go of everyone who had been involved in it. I found myself asking Jesus why He had allowed this to happen to me, to which He said He was right there and that He had kept me. The forgiveness and release session took hours with a lot of wriggling on the floor, crying and screaming from the pain. It felt as though there was something being detached from my insides. There, was a separation that was happening. I assume that there was a stronghold, or spirits, that had attached themselves to me because of the wound, that open door.

Therefore, I would experience all the misfortunes. I do not dismiss that the enemy could have been attacking me in other ways. However, if there was nothing in me that identified with him then his work would have not been effective. I was healed of the shame, betrayal, rejection, bitterness, and all suppressed emotions received healing. That day was the beginning of the healing of my soul and life. I began to experience prosperity in my soul, which then began to effortlessly overflow to my life in the natural. These healing sessions with the Holy Spirit gave me skills in effective forgiveness, letting go and inner healing. Now I understand that it is important for one's soul to be healed because that is the seat of everything that happens in one's life. The Bible says above all else, guard your heart for everything you do flows from it **(Proverbs 4:23)**.

If we want to experience joy and everything we have been created to have, then we also need to be diligent with our hearts and address those issues that seem insignificant in our present moment. The way one can see that there is something controlling their lives even though it happened years ago is a dig in the unconscious mind. Are there any thoughts that spring up when something happens, when something is said or when you go to a place? Does a present hurt connect with a scenario or hurt in the past? Do you feel emotional pain in the heart, stomach or palm of the hand? Frequent nightmares are also an indicator that something is not okay. It depends on the person's processing; to some people it could show as depression, anger, jealous, alcohol, drugs, promiscuity, hiding and feeling afraid, shame, guilt or timidity.

The cure for issues like these, in most instances, is letting go of the past and extending the hand of forgiveness, which leads to inner wholeness and healing. An understanding of forgiveness is paramount because this enables one to begin to deal with these wounds. Forgiveness is a deliberate conscious decision to release feelings of resentment or vengeance toward a person or a group who has harmed you whether they deserve it or not. In other words, forgiveness is a choice that you the wounded makes. It is not dependent on the perpetrator. The ultimate goal for forgiveness and letting go is for your freedom and happiness. When one is in denial of what happened and how it made them feel they will find it hard to receive healing because they choose to disassociate with what is present in their unconscious mind. This journey of healing developed in me compassion, love, and the desire to assist other people who have vicious cycles in life. I am on a mission to see people's souls prosper. I can easily pick a wounded heart just by having a 10-minute conversation with a person. I see this as a gift God has given me to walk with others on a journey of healing.

Forgiveness is something that everyone in the world needs to do because we all get wounded when things happen in life. The God who created us is the one who showed this attribute towards us and taught us the importance of walking it. Forgiveness is talked about a lot in religious circles. However, there also needs to be an effective way of helping people on how to do it and show people its importance. I have coached and mentored people who have found it difficult to forgive because they felt the other person or group would be winning or held on to unforgiveness because they waited for an apology. This is a misunderstanding on what forgiveness is all about. Forgiveness is for our own hearts; it heals us and not the perpetrator.

I was healed because I said yes to forgiveness, the wound was not only closed but it was eradicated together with everything that had settled on it. My life began to change and make sense, the confusion I carried for years was removed; I saw a brighter day. I started opening and trusting again. We need to take ownership of our wounds and choose to walk in forgiveness so that our lives prosper.

2
Before
I
Became

LAURENCIA SOLOMON

LAURENCIA was a typical daddy's girl and everything she asked for, she received... My daddy was my first love and my all. Life was so perfect so I carried this notion with me until one dark morning... On March 25, 2004 I received a telephone call that my daddy had passed on. Something just died in me. I did not care about anything anymore because the one person who was my 'everything', the one I lived to impress, was no more. The person who once told me, "Even if I am dead and I hear your name, I will wake up" was gone. I believed him when I was a little innocent girl, oh bless my heart! I started to reflect upon some of the advice my daddy used to give me in his commemoration, such as, nothing is permanent in this world and so I should be able to adjust to any situation or condition I found myself in. Indeed, nothing, either good or bad, is permanent!

Fast forward... Married, with three wonderful children in America. Oh! Boy! America was no exception. I lived in a beautiful five bedroom newly built home. Life could not have been better because anytime I had a baby, my car would be changed or upgraded. After my third child, I decided it was time to move back to the United Kingdom as I was more interested in the British educational system. Moreover, it was an opportunity for me to continue with my education. Therefore, in 2006 I moved back to the UK from America to achieve my plans, not knowing what lay ahead of us.

Indeed, no situation is permanent! We had to live with a friend upon arriving in the UK. I began assessing the system of my rights as a British-born citizen so that I could settle well. One morning, I dressed up the children and went to the council office. My hopes were so high that I could get housed the very same day because I had three children and I felt that they could understand the situation; that it was not convenient living in a room in a friend's house with the children. However, to my surprise, I was told by the council that they could only house me, and not the children because they did not hold British passports. I was shocked because I thought my children would be British if I was! My heart was broken and so devastated that day, but I did not give up. In this case, giving up was not an option.

The next morning, my friend took me to the Citizen Advisory Bureau, and I believe that the advisor I met that faithful day was as destiny helper. He assured me that he would help me. I believe he could see my worry and confusion. Without wasting time, he grabbed pen and paper, and started explaining how my children were British, quoting laws that supported his argument, and he also included how my parents had worked and paid taxes in the country etc.

However, I was advised to quickly apply for British passports for the children as I sent the letter to the council office. The passports would serve as evidence for the children's entitlement. I heeded the advice and within one week, I went to London because the person who was supposed to sign the children's passports was there. As a result, I got the passports within two weeks. This meant that I now had my evidence, and I went back to the council office and presented the passports so that they could include the children on the application.

The council office updated my records and included my children in my application but did not offer me housing because they said I was not homeless, although I had explained to them I was living in a single room in a friend's house. I was gutted, in the country I called home, and where I was a citizen by birth? As much as you can be close to someone and love each other, sometimes when one overstays their welcome there can be issues that arise. I had my own family in another family home. Tensions began to rise. Although my friend and her husband had really shown us love by housing us, it was becoming so difficult, and it made me uncomfortable, as it was uncomfortable for them as well. In our past conversations, my friend and I had discussed that the council was more lenient to those who absolutely had nowhere to live so the best thing I could do was pack my bags out of the house and take the children to the council so I could declare myself homeless. Though my friend was not entirely pleased with this, I had no choice but I was adamant to make a life for my family.

The housing officer interviewed and registered me, but he made me aware that they had no house available at that time. This was another obstacle. However, I was given a place in a women's shelter and I was so shocked because I never thought it would come to this! Living in a women's shelter! In the process of this blow in my face, I remembered what my father used to say to me, and I consented to the available accommodation they were offering me. They made the contact and gave me the address of the shelter. When I came out of the office, I told my friend what had happened; she felt so bad and told me that I was still welcome in her house. She then drove us to the shelter. They registered us and showed us our room, and I had not been told that it was not free. I had to pay with my benefits of which I had not even received.

As soon as I entered the room, I lost all control of my emotions. I was all over the place. I did not know how to express how I was feeling; hysterical, distraught. I just cried. My then five-year-old daughter asked me, "Mum, why are we here?" That statement propelled me to the next level of my confusion. I wept. I was so sick to the pit of my stomach. My children also started crying. I had to stop weeping and pull myself together and explain to them what was really happening and the process of quickly getting a house. The room had two bunk beds. I cannot recall if there were pillows but the whole place was smelling of cigarettes and the carpet was so filthy. It looked like it had not been washed in decades. It was inhuman to think that room was suitable for someone to sleep in. The whole place was just not up to human standards.

Thank God, we made it through the night. In the morning, I called my friend to help me take my daughter to school because it was far from the shelter. Later I decided to get a small car because I felt like I was inconveniencing my friend. Having a car in a way lifted some of the burden that came with the situation. One day I went to the reception to check if they had heard anything about housing me. The lady at the reception said they had not found anything yet. She asked me, "Do you know you can find private housing and the government will pay for it? Because waiting for a house from the council would take longer."

I did not have an idea so she helped me with some details. I was so excited as if I had already got the house. I started house hunting. Little did I know that property owners did not like housing DSS tenants, meaning no unemployed council tenants because, apart from the stigma attached to it, property owners always had problems with such tenants. For me this was another obstacle. But I continued to search. I never gave up. I then found a house and the landlady was willing to accept a DSS tenant with the condition of one month deposit and two months' rent. I took it. I moved into the house, and bought few essentials. Just when I had settled in, the landlady started complaining here and there about unnecessary things. I was tired of her complaints before six months. I decided to start the search again. However, this time it was easier because I had a reference from my previous landlady. Everything went through smoothly then I moved into my second house within eight months. The house was nice.

However, I was still uneasy because of my previous experience. After about two months, I started feeling relaxed and my children were happy with the house and so I made it a home for them. We were settled!

While I was going through all this, for some strange reason, I ceased communication with my family. I did not know why but I guess I wanted to do this alone to prove a point that I could make it on my own. That was because nearly all my life, I had been considered a "daddy's girl". At this point, I did not have a relationship with God even though I had grown up in a strong Catholic home. I was just lost! Occasionally, I would drink wine and sleep. I do not remember praying once but God still loved and sustained me, as the Bible says in **Romans 5:6-8**, *"For when we were still without strength, in due time Christ died for the ungodly. For scarcely for a righteous man will one die; yet perhaps for a good man someone would even dare to die. But God demonstrates His own love toward us, in that while we were still sinners, Christ died for us."* **(NKJV).**

Life was starting to become meaningful again, so I went to Wolverhampton College to enrol for an academic course. They assessed and helped me to start a Diploma in Business Administration. I had been last in education when I was in secondary school in Ghana. A friend and I had discussed about going to school, but she recommended that I just had to focus on getting a decent job instead of wasting my time in going to school. However, I discovered that she herself was completing a nursing degree. It puzzled me why then she would discourage me to do the very same thing she was doing. Nevertheless, I continued with my plans. At this time, I had two older children in primary school and my last in the nursery and so every morning I would drop off my children and then go to college.

I remember the first day. I was so overwhelmed with excitement and at the same time proud of myself. I enjoyed the course and decided that I was not going to give up. We sometimes got assignments to work in groups and it was a blessing that I met two people who were from Ghana as well. This made me so comfortable, and we became casual friends. The lady invited me to their church so I could worship with them, but I told her that I did not go to church. She was being kind to me, but I was not in that frame of mind yet.

College continued as normal until the day I had one of my exams. As my traditional routine dictated, I left home to drop off my children. Upon reaching the primary school, I discovered it was closed. "I have an exam!" I exclaimed to myself. I had forgotten about the half term; I had been faced with another obstacle because I had nowhere to take the children so l could go and write the exam. So, I took the children with me to the college and explained my situation to my tutor. She assured me not to worry and rang the college nursery so they could help me with childcare as I wrote the exam. When I returned to college the next day, my tutor called me for a discussion pertaining the previous incident. She was worried about what had happened and so she asked me, "all your three children are under ten and you are doing college all by yourself? How do you do it? I just said I did not know but for some reason, I was doing it. At that time, l did not have a relationship with God but He still looked after me. His word in **Jeremiah 29:11 (NKJV)** said, *"For I know the thoughts that I think toward you, says the* Lord, *thoughts of peace and not of evil, to give you a **future** and a **hope**."*

Then she said, "*Wow!*" She wished me every success in the future and to keep the positivity so I would go far. A few months later in June, I completed college successfully. I enrolled again and waited to start my degree in Business Management and Human Resources in September. But during the waiting period, I felt a void inside me. At first, I thought it was because I was not going to college anymore. After dropping off my children, I would usually go to the shopping centre to window shop till school finished. I did this a few times but still felt the same. I drank more wine, and nothing changed. The void continued for a while but one fine evening I was watching television, suddenly, I felt darkness, thick darkness... I do not know how to describe it. Then I asked myself why didn't I have a Bible in the house?

I searched on eBay and found one, but waiting for three days for it to be delivered would have been too long for me. I wanted a Bible at that very moment. That night was so long for me. I just wanted a Bible; I could not wait to go out to the shopping centre to buy one.

I did my morning school run and went straight to the book shop and asked for a Bible. I was filled with so much joy when I held that £5 Bible in my hands. Indeed, for *"Many are called, but few are chosen." **(Matthew 22:14, NKJV)***. When I received the invitation from the lady I met in college I declined, but when my time was up, I was arrested by the Holy Spirit himself. Later that evening, I opened the Bible and started flipping the pages. I did not even know what I was doing then again it occurred to me to look for the popular verses I knew from childhood (John 2:16, Psalm 23, etc.). I began feeling excited! *"Train up a child in the way they should go, And when he is old he will not depart from it."* ***(Proverbs 22:6 NKJV)***.

Despite the excitement of having a Bible I still felt something needed to be fulfilled in me. It was not owning the Bible that was so important. It was reading it. Moreover, I had no clue on how to navigate through it. I also struggled with praying; I was ashamed to pray aloud, so I only settled to praying in my head. Oh, my goodness when the Holy Spirit is on your case, He will not stop until what He needs from you is done! He made me remember the lady from those days in college. I looked for her contact details and inquired of her church address and that weekend I joined her in fellowship as she had invited me before. I was really blessed when I went to church that day. The people were welcoming and lovely. Since that day I have never stopped attending the church.

I started university and things were good but physically I found it hard raising three children all under 10 years while studying full time. This became draining because I had to cater for the children when I got home and make sure they were settled in bed. After all the evening chores were done, I would have time for myself. I did my assignments sometimes until 2 to 3am with exception of Fridays when I would retire to bed at 6am for a good three years while studying for my degree. Moreover, I decided to get myself a part time job because the student finance was not enough for me. I was working with an employment agency and I would pick shifts that worked around university. The good thing at that time was that we had a church family that also had their children in the same school as my children. They helped me with picking my children from school. My job was seasonal. It meant that it would end when the contract finished, which is what happened, and I continued looking for a job.

I continued searching for jobs, I was also in my final year in University, during this time my spiritual life was all right, going to church almost every Sunday and started knowing people, my children made friends and so they were happy to attend church. In 2012, I graduated from university, I needed employment urgently since student finance was going to stop. I do not remember how many job application rejections I got. However, that week in church we had a visiting pastor and he called for seed sowing for a particular need, I went for it, but it was more a let me try and see thing, the pastor said pray over your seed tell God what you want, and He will do it. A few weeks later, I got a job interview via an agency, the agency booked an appointment for me to have a pre-interview with them, my interviewer was so nice, he encouraged me and said to me if you go for the interview and you perform like you have done today, there is no doubt you will get the job.

The day of the interview came, and I went with so much confidence, it went very well, and I was told that they would get back to me shortly. Four or five days later, the telephone call I was waiting for came, and I was not successful because they felt my qualification was higher than the position available. I did not understand because I was under the impression that it was a good thing for the organisation. I was so disappointed. However, I kept on applying for jobs. Within a week or so I received another call from the agency for a different job application, and booked a pre-interview again. Most of the time agencies hide the organisation's identity, so I was reluctant to attend this time but then again, I went and to my surprise, I met the same person I had met for the previous pre-interview. Then I got to know it is the same organisation who had rejected me but now a different department. We went through the usual drill. I noticed that the man was not himself because he did not say much but just wished me good luck. I was uncomfortable and was contemplating whether to go for the interview or not. The interview went well, and this time the interviewer said "see you soon". I was not convinced, but when I came out of the building, I looked back and said, "This is where I belong."

In three days, I received a call that let me know that I got the job. I did not believe it until the lady who called asked me if I was not happy that I got the job. Then I shouted, "Jesus!" This was a happy moment for me. I graduated in May 2012 and was employed in June 2012 and this position was not even close to what I had studied in university. However, this was a full-time job. I desperately took a full-time job without thinking of how I was going to manage with my children. I contacted the family from church who had helped me previously with my children, and, thank God, they accepted to help in any way they could. I thank God that they became a solution in my situation. I started working and so I would drop off the children in the morning, park in the children's school and take the tram to work a distance of about 40 – 45 minutes from the school. I worked from 9am to 4:30pm, and was constantly running to and from work because if I missed the tram. I would be late to work and I had always wanted to pick up my children as soon as possible from the family friends. This struggle was real. It caught up with me. I was running late to work almost every other day. My manager spoke to me to find out what was happening. I explained the tram situation to her, and she told me that I could change my start time and be careful because managers would start keeping records of lateness.

I had to make some changes before I lose the job, so I adjusted my time of waking up and the pressure was eased off a bit. However, anytime I heard half-term or insert day. My heart will skip a beat as

I had not been employed for that long to accumulate holidays. I was so desperate. I sat my children down and spoke to them that I had to work and so come half term, I needed their help and they agreed. After the agreement, before I left for work, I would bring everything I thought they would need upstairs and plead with them to stay upstairs. Normally they would be sleeping when I left. I used to sneak out of my home so that the neighbours would not notice that I had left the children alone. My heart will be in my stomach till I return from work and if I see a call from them, I would panic that something may have happened.

On one such occasion, I received a call from home. Ah! God, my daughter was on the phone crying. I told my manager I needed to go home. I came home and my daughter had a split toe, and there was blood everywhere. She said as they were playing, her brother stepped on her toes. I took her to the hospital, and they dressed it and we came home. The next day I decided to stay home but my daughter wept and begged me to go to work because she did not want to be the cause of losing my job and this was barely one month on the job. I left for work with tears in my eyes. I returned home that evening, on July 25, 2012 and I found this letter, no name, no address:

Hello

I write to express my concerns to you about leaving your three very young children home alone for very long periods of time. Whilst it is not illegal to leave your child home alone, providing they are mentally capable of dealing with emergencies, leaving a young child under the age of 16 to care for other children is not alright. Even more so when they are all of primary school age. When the NSPCC are informed of any children left home alone, they will normally involve the police fast then the police involve child services. I would not like to think that you would return home to find your children have been taken into care without giving you the opportunity to put things right by finding appropriate care for your children whilst you are out. I will be back in your area on Friday morning. If I do not see any improvements, I will have no other alternative but to contact the NSPCC."

I am yet to find this person another obstacle! My children and I wept so badly that we could not eat that night, I then had to contact people from the church to see if they could help me babysit my children. I got some help, people were willing to help me as and when necessary. I cried almost every evening until I could find a babysitter for my children, but there were times they could not help. I perfectly understood because personally. I did not like bothering people with my problems, so I found an after-school club that charged £44 a day. And I was earning about £43 a day, so it was making a strain on my finances. I went to work and asked my manager if it was possible for me to change my shift to part-time. She took it forward, then a few months later, I was granted 25 hours per week and I was also able to book my annual leave around half term. I had a breathing space, and my children were growing.

As crazy and determined as I am, I decided to go back to school for my Masters' degree programme on a part-time basis. Back then, funding was not available, so I spoke to my bank, and they approved it. I enrolled in Human Resource Management, went for induction only for my bank to tell me that I did not qualify for the post-graduate loan. I had to drop out of university with a pile of debts. After a year or two, I went back. It also came with its challenges; this time there were more obstacles. Although I could not take rejection and failure, I stepped back and focused more on my children, church, and the charity I had always wanted. Work was fine, I had been made a permanent employee, but I was still not satisfied. I started feeling sad and, strangely, I chanced on a pastor on FB preaching on purpose in life. It resonated with me and so I started on my purpose journey; what is my purpose on this earth? I researched it, and the results were not satisfying (people were talking about the things you do effortlessly is your purpose) but with me, there are a lot of things I do effortlessly if I put my mind to it so I was not happy with that.

I decided to talk to God about this. I took two weeks' annual leave from work and started praying and fasting about this void, and when I went to sleep, God would show me things in my dreams and I received prophecies from pastors, too. I continued to pray, and I felt my relationship with God become stronger. I was seeing visions, feeling other people's emotions, going into trance, having deep dreams and all I wanted to do was to spend more time with God. Amazing experiences! As time went on, I started developing a deep interest in going back to school to study LL.M in international law. While doing the charity, and baking, I enrolled for the course. This time I had managed to get funding for study, and I even got my first module free. I started my charity All Community Network Projects (ACN) and organised a youth conference to help them discover their purpose. I started baking more and more. It was true I experienced what **Matthew 6:33 (NKJV)** says, *"But seek first the kingdom of God and His righteousness, and all these things shall be added to you."* Everything fitted into place like a puzzle, indeed, *"He has made everything beautiful in its time." **(Ecclesiastes 3:11 NKJV).***

By God's grace and mercies. My children have grown up beautifully, and I am still working for the same organisation full time again nine years on, still doing charity, a self-taught baker now a businesswoman, a preacher, an intercessor, a worshiper, a speaker, an entrepreneur etc. My slogan is 'A banker by day, a baker by night.'

I have read the Bible and the amazing testimonies in there and I have always wanted my testimony, THIS IS MY BIBLE STORY! Now, I do not look back, the only time I look back is to check how far God has brought me.

I pray that as you read my test, my testimony, it inspires and encourages you to never give up in life no matter the challenges. Bear in mind, giving up does not exist in your book! I know everybody's test is different that is what makes God wonderful. Remember, *"No temptation has overtaken you except such as is common to man; but God is faithful, who will not allow you to be tempted beyond what you are able, but with the temptation will also make the way of escape, that you may be able to bear it." (1 Corinthians 10:13, NKJV).*

Do not allow anybody to put you down, you can do anything you want to do once you do not give up, because anytime you believe in yourself, you become God in action, He created you in His own image, think about it, this means anytime you see your picture it is God you are seeing.

His grace is sufficient for YOU TOO!

3
Focus
On the Journey, not the
Distractions

ADESUWA OMOREGIE OGIE

Always remember, your focus determines your reality. —
George Lucy

I HAVE always had a tendency of seeing tasks through. I remember during my school days; I would stay up all night studying with the most serious boys in class. Although I achieved good grades, unfortunately, I couldn't get into the higher institution of my choice due to flaws in the education system. I needed more than good grades to qualify and the financial difficulties made it impossible to continue.

After a while, I had an opportunity to travel to Europe but encountered a lot of difficulties on the way. However, I focused on the fact that it was all working for my good and made the best of every situation without allowing the difficulties to define me.

As we journey through our time here on earth, there is a need to resolve that no matter what, you must keep your head up. Remembering my earlier years in Europe, as young people, we enjoyed ourselves by going out drinking. However, I realised that was something that could deviate my attention and lure me into an unpalatable lifestyle. Therefore, I made a decision not to entangle myself but it was not easy, as peer pressure was a serious reality. Nevertheless, allowing any form of distraction could weaken my resolve to succeed.

As explained earlier, there are obstacles in life that can taint our resolve to be focused. I was often disappointed and lamented how life was unfair and cruel. Yet God sees the end of a thing from the beginning. He had His eyes on me, according to His word in ***Isaiah 43:2 (KJV)***, *"When thou passest through the waters, I will be with thee; and through the rivers, they shall not overflow thee: when thou walkest through the fire, thou shalt not be burned, neither shall the flame kindle upon thee. 3 For I am Jehovah thy God, the Holy One of Israel, thy Saviour; I have given Egypt as thy ransom, Ethiopia and Seba in thy stead. 4 Since thou hast been precious in my sight, [and] honourable, and I have loved thee; therefore will I give men in thy stead, and peoples instead of thy life. 5 Fear not; for I am with thee: I will bring thy seed from the east, and gather thee from the west;"*

God was in it with me even when I couldn't sense it and he was by my side. One of my earliest jobs was tough and far from what I had dreamt. However, I was determined to grow in and through it by making the best of my situation fulfilling the saying that when the desirable is not available, the available becomes desirable. I worked hard in that company from the bottom pushing all the way through to the top. It was a big hospitality company with various restaurants and I started off as a dishwasher but I wanted to become a chef. There were various obstacles in my way to achieving this dream. This included a language barrier, so I had to make great effort to learn the language (Spanish) as all the menus in the restaurants were written in Spanish. I also had to go through professional training going from one stage to the other for my work. I also began to voluntarily come in two hours every day before my start time to gain extra skills that would cover up for what I lacked.

I was raising a young family in a foreign land but the Lord was with me. He was taking me to my desired destination, prepared for me before the beginning of time. I can relate to the story of Joseph who saw the dream the Lord had for him but circumstances and other people's influence caused detours and delays. Yet there was no denial from the God who sees us and preserve us for His glory.

Joseph was focused irrespective of the challenges and obstacles and because his heart was pure and fixed on the dream God showed him, God preserved him. Joseph had very peculiar dreams that he was going to be a ruler over his brothers and even his parents would be under his reign. This didn't sit well with those that heard it and plans were put in place to eliminate him. **Genesis 37:5 (KJV)**, *"And Joseph dreamed a dream, and he told it to his brethren: and they hated him yet the more. 6 And he said unto them, Hear, I pray you, this dream which I have dreamed: 7 for, behold, we were binding sheaves in the field, and, lo, my sheaf arose, and also stood upright; and, behold, your sheaves came round about, and made obeisance to my sheaf. 8 And his brethren said to him, Shalt thou indeed reign over us? Or shalt thou indeed have dominion over us? And they hated him yet the more for his dreams, and for his words. 9 And he dreamed yet another dream, and told it to his brethren, and said, Behold, I have dreamed yet a dream: and, behold, the sun and the moon and eleven stars made obeisance to me. 10 And he told it to his father, and to his brethren; and his father rebuked him, and said unto him, what is this dream that thou hast dreamed? Shall I and thy mother and thy brethren indeed come to bow down ourselves to thee to the earth? 11 And his brethren envied him; but his father kept the saying in mind."*

Just like you and I, Joseph had dreams of who God had called him to be and, like us, he had to go through hurdles, setbacks, pitfalls, disappointments and betrayals. He also encountered unfair situations and circumstances. Joseph was destined to be a leader but as we go through his life story, we find out that his life was threatened, he was kidnapped and made as a slave. Later, he was falsely accused of sexual assault and eventually became a prisoner. Yet through this process something stands out about Joseph that we could all learn from — his focus!

I define focus as the staying ability to see a particular goal through, no matter the odds against it. The dictionary describes it as the state or quality of having or producing clear visual definition. As children of God, the Lord encourages us to focus on Christ our Saviour, the Author and finisher of the faith we profess. **Hebrews 12:2-3 (KJV)**, *"Fixing our eyes on Jesus, the pioneer and perfecter of faith. Who for the joy set before him he endured the cross, scorning its shame, and sat down at the right hand of the throne of God. Consider him who endured such opposition from sinners, so that you will not grow weary and lose heart."*

During times of trial in our lives, it's difficult to understand what God is doing. It seems even the enemy will be rejoicing that he has the upper hand but it eludes him that our God specialises in turning trials to triumph and tests to testimonies. He uses the challenges to prune and groom us. God also refines us like gold and silver that has to pass through the fire to be rid of all impurities. This is in order to be fit for purpose like ornaments and jewellery of great value. The Bible says in the master's house there are vessels of wood and clay and vessels of silver and gold. Vessels unto honour and dishonour. For us to able to represent the Father with empathy and compassion, he sometimes allows circumstances to prune us, ground us and mould us into that version of Himself he wants to showcase in and through our lives. So let us always remember that God in His infinite wisdom will not leave us nor forsake us, no matter how difficult and dark it seems.

Joseph was a focused young man so that even in the most trying times in his life, he was still exhibiting leadership qualities. As a slave, he was the head and executed his work with excellence. As a prisoner, his excellent qualities were not overlooked. No matter our circumstances, we should not lose focus on who we are and what we are able to offer even when these situations are below our intended preferences. We must learn to handle them without bitterness or evil disposition but with a cheerful heart and a spirit of excellence.

As mentioned before, I also learned to focus on my work and eventually made a career of it. During my time on the job, my language skills improved tremendously.

As time went on, my relationship with the Lord was also getting serious, as He drew me nearer to Him and I became more aware of His presence. In my church, a need arose for an interpreter, to interpret the pastor's message to the national language of Spanish. To my surprise, I was approached and appointed for that role. Who would have envisaged that a skill learnt for a secular job and for survival would be useful for kingdom purposes? My excellent language skills became an opportunity for the Lord to teach me His Word and His ways. As mentioned earlier, focus is very crucial if we are to excel in any given assignment. I was resolved to do an excellent job of it, so I started studying and learning the deep biblical meanings of the words. Studying the scripture in another language proved more challenging than I would have expected or imagined but I was determined!

Prior to this time, a surprising incident happened in my church that opened the door to new possibilities. A guest speaker that had been scheduled to come dropped out at the last minute and we were stuck. So, I suggested that we should do it ourselves but no one was willing to take up the task. Public speaking wasn't my cup of tea at all and I often avoided testifying publicly so giving the speech would definitely be a great challenge. In spite of my reservations about it, I volunteered to be the speaker and it was met with mockery and ridicule by the team. Instead of allowing that to dampen my interest, it actually fuelled my resolve to take up the speaking assignment and to my amazement and that of my hearers, it went very well. This incident gave my confidence a boost to take up the opportunity to become an interpreter as well as more teaching and preaching assignments which sharpened my speaking skills. I was focused on the journey, irrespective of all the challenges and obstacles.

*A clear vision backed up by definite plan gives you a tremendous feeling of confidence and personal power — **Brian Tracy.***

My confidence soared with every opportunity to practice in my new assignment. As I gave it my all, I discovered my relevance to certain groups of people in the church increased as I became the go to person for their consultation. This led me to be more involved with the leadership and management of the church activities which in turn placed a greater demand of spiritual responsibility. God was at work all the time, pruning, teaching, empowering, moulding and building me for the purpose ahead and because I was focused on making the best of my situation, I was in agreement with His plans and purpose for me.

Our focus really will determine our reality. God is ever faithful; nothing catches Him by surprise. Your present situation and circumstances do not throw Him off balance. Those betrayals, disappointments, ill-treatment, misunderstandings and misconceptions put in place to discourage and deviate our destinies are the same tools He will use to propel us into that place He has prepared for us to manifest His glory. Joseph told his brothers, you meant this for evil but God knew it before hand and has prepared it for good. ***Genesis 50:19**, "But Joseph said to them, 'Don't be afraid. Am I in the place of God? 20 You intended to harm me, but God intended it for good to accomplish what is now being done, the **saving** of many lives. God knows and rules in the affairs of man, He turns situation around for our good and to glorify His name in our lives."*

Remember, our focus should always be on who God has desired us to be from the beginning irrespective of the hiccups and stumbling blocks in our way. We must also maintain a pure heart allowing God's will to prevail at all times.

Romans 12:16, *"Live in harmony with one another. Do not be proud, but be willing to associate with people of low position. Do not be conceited. 17 Do not repay anyone evil for evil. Be careful to do what is right in the eyes of everyone. 18 If it is possible, as far as it depends on* *you, live at peace with everyone. 19 Do not take revenge, my dear friends, but leave room for God's wrath, for it is written: 'It is mine to avenge; I will repay,' says the Lord. 20 On the contrary: 'If your enemy is hungry, feed him; if he is thirsty, give him something to drink. In doing this, you will heap burning coals on his head.' 21 Do not be overcome by evil, but overcome evil with good."*

Allowing God's word to have its way in my heart has helped me eliminate unnecessary distractions and negative energy but instead focusing on what God was doing, it brings understanding to my heart, opening eyes to see beyond the obvious and empowering me to soar over storms of life that would have otherwise break me or overwhelmed me.

Determination with Wisdom

As I grow in the things of God, I realised that in God we all are designed for purpose but it takes determination, wisdom and focus to stay on the path and align ourselves with God's divine purpose. In everything, seeking God's heart and mind is very important. The book of Proverbs admonishes us to not lean on our own understanding but commit all our endeavours into the able hands of God. **Proverbs 3:5**, *"Trust in the Lord with all your heart and lean not on your own understanding; 6 in all your ways submit to him, and he will make your paths straight."*

Living and working in a place where I had to learn a different language and working below my expectations wasn't a walk in the park but in retrospect, I realised that it was all intentionally orchestrated to build me up for the assignment ahead of me. The time in my workplace did not only equip me with culinary skills but also wider and more complex people skills. This included liaising with foreigners from different walks of life who were first generation immigrants looking for greener pastures and like myself wary of the unknown and the uncertainty of their future. This common and shared concern brought us together and gave me extra opportunities for evangelism, slowly solidifying my calling.

I am thankful for the gift, focus and determination to push through, no matter what, because our God is able to do more abundantly that we can ever imagine. He used all my experiences and my location for the propagation of the kingdom. After many years in Spain, I moved to the UK and guess what? My ears were instinctively attuned to Spanish-speaking individuals! I was burdened in my spirit to reach out to them and befriend them, evangelising to them and their families. God moved in such an awesome way that deliverance, healing and restoration of faith was so evident. Some of them got strengthened by God such that they were able to evangelise in their community. As a result, they were able to have their own cell group for Bible study, which I supported for a number of years, all in the Spanish language that had been such a challenge to me years back.

Seeing what the Lord has done and is still doing in the midst of these wonderful people, I can testify that God's thoughts towards us are of good and not evil to give us purpose and a future in him. **Jeremiah 29:11**, *"For I know the plans I have for you,' declares the Lord, 'plans to prosper you and not to harm you, plans to give you hope and a future.'"*

Lessons on Focus

What is our pursuit? God's perfect will for us. **Matthew 6:33**, *But seek ye first the kingdom of God, and his righteousness; and all these things shall be added unto you.*

No matter what comes against you or your purpose, remember to make the best of every situation without taking your eyes off the desired destination. What the Lord has prepared you is greater than the enemy trying to derail you.

1 John 4:4, *You, dear children, are from God and have overcome them, because the one who is in you is greater than the one who is in the world.*

Along with a strong belief in your own inner voice, you also need laser-like focus combined with unwavering determination. — **Larry Flint**

Believe in the voice of God inside of you that is propelling you into your calling. Never second-guess yourself nor doubt but believe He can turn any situation around for your good and to the glory of His Holy Name. ***Mark 9:23***, *Jesus said unto him, If thou canst believe, all things are possible to him that believe.*

Do it! People who succeed don't just sit and think about what they want to do. They take meaningful, purposeful, directional action consistently and persistently. Every step they take puts them toward the outcome they're looking for. — **Dr Phil.**

Joseph was still working every day in the prison yet circumstances didn't change his focus. He even asked the baker to remember him when he gained his freedom. Being intentional and tenacious in the pursuit of a desired result will keep us focused.

May the fear of the Lord ground us and may His wisdom direct us through it all. ***Proverbs 2:2-7 (KJV)***, *So that thou incline thine ear unto wisdom, and apply thine heart to understanding; 3 Yea, if thou criest after knowledge, and liftest up thy voice for understanding; 4 If thou seekest her as silver, and searchest for her as for hid treasures; 5 Then shalt thou understand the fear of the LORD, and find the knowledge of God. 6 For the LORD giveth wisdom: out of his mouth cometh knowledge and understanding. 7 He layeth up sound wisdom for the righteous: he is a buckler to them that walk uprightly.*

Work with enthusiasm and passion because service equals relevance. ***Ecclesiastes 9:10 (KJV)***, *Whatsoever thy hand findeth to do,* *do it with thy might; for there is no work, nor device, nor knowledge, nor wisdom, in the grave, whither thou goest.*

Being determined means being single minded. Remember you have a purpose to fulfil and everything you do should be channelled towards that. **Proverbs 4:24 (KJV)**, *Put away from thee a froward mouth, and perverse lips put far from thee. 25 Let thine eyes look right on, and let thine eyelids look straight before thee. 26 Ponder the path of thy feet, and let all thy ways be established. 27 Turn not to the right hand nor to the left: remove thy foot from evil.*

Your life is controlled by what you focus on — **Tony Robbins.**

Philippians 4:8 (KJV), *Finally, brethren, whatsoever things are true, whatsoever things are honest, whatsoever things are just, whatsoever things are pure, whatsoever things are lovely, whatsoever things are of good report; if there be any virtue, and if there be any praise, think on these things.*

Prayer

Heavenly Father, thank you for your love and thoughts towards us. Thank you for your Spirit that guides us into all truth, and always prompts us towards your will and purpose for us. As we continue to desire to do your will, help us to focus on your promises. Let the entrance of your Word be our guide. Lead us beside still waters and restore our weary souls. As we emerge into all you have purposed us to be, help us to be grounded in you and for you. Bring to our remembrance that our life is hidden in you and all that we are is because you are. Thank you, Father, for making us partakers of your inheritance with the saints in Jesus' mighty name. Amen.

4

Prayer
Master Key that Unlocks
Doors

CHIEDZA NYAKUWA

THIS is an encouragement that I write from my heart, dedicated to those that are broken. I am married with two beautiful children and I live in Chitungwiza, Zimbabwe. I am writing to encourage readers, anyone who is broken and believes their world is crumbling or has crumbled, that God is not dead. He works in mysterious ways. I have had an encounter with the Lord. He has been very faithful to me, and I feel compelled to share my journey.

The Lord has done innumerable things in my life. I cannot imagine my life without such a loving God. There are times you experience a lot of hardships and you ask: "Lord, where are you?" But He's not far away; He's always close by. As I was growing up, my father secretly struggled with ill-health. It never showed outwardly because he masked it so well. It was not widely talked about, but as his family, we knew he did not have a clean bill of health. He had a good job that he loved dearly. We were all used to his situation. We made it part of him. In fact, we normalised it as part of his health.

My father used to love the bottle. I remember one day I asked him if ever he was going to quit drinking; and he responded with a loud laugh, "Never!" We both laughed our lungs out because, though sad, his response was coloured with humour. Whenever he drank, his legs would swell because he had gout and arthritis but that didn't seem strong enough to deter him. He was set in his ways. My brother and I would put ice blocks round it.

Every Sunday, we would all go to church; he was a very good singer. My mum and he were both in the church choir. They enjoyed singing. Every day before we went to bed, we would sing, read the Bible and then pray. We were only two children, my brother and I, so my dad chose me to be his prayer partner while my mum chose my brother.

We were good together as prayer partners. There was a time when I was job hunting and he helped me pray to get a job. I was invited for an interview. After three days, I was told I had been successful. Immediately, I called my dad to break the good news to him. We both wept on the phone, knowing that God had come through for us.

Those were tears of joy! We spent a few minutes crying and he gathered courage and prayed before we ended the conversation. When I got home, we all celebrated. However, the joy expressed was much more obvious with my dad and myself; because we had called on God together and he answered our prayers.

The reality of Dad's failing health made life a bit uncertain! I remember when I was 28. One day while taking a bath and imagined my future wedding; I wondered what it would be like, or planned in my fantasies how it should play out in real life. Knowing my dad was not always in good health, I asked God to have my dad walk me down the aisle. Rather than him being just my dad, my request to God was more so... as he was my prayer partner, my friend. Above all, I had a strong desire for my loving dad to be able to enjoy my wedding despite the illness. I also prayed that he would see my first child and get to play with his grandchild — and enjoy each other's company.

The following year, my husband proposed, and we laid out a plan for the traditional engagement. He visited my family so that final arrangements could be made. He came to pay *lobola*.[1] After the bride price negotiations, my husband's family indicated they wanted us to have a white wedding but, unfortunately, they didn't have money for it, so we decided to shelve the wedding to a later time. However, dad said he would have none of that, and directed that in three weeks' time, his son-in-law and daughter would be tying the knot. I was a bit upset with him and wondered why he was being so upfront when our coffers were dry. When my in-laws had left, all he said to me was that God would provide.

At that time, it did not make sense to me — to wed in three weeks with no money to bankroll the nuptials was not practical. I just took his word, though, because he was my dad; I could not argue with him. My mother went round the neighbourhood telling people that I would be getting married. The announcement was made by word of mouth because we did not even have money for the invitation cards. I thought that was very embarrassing! Why were we forcing matters!

In the first two weeks, we prayed about it as a family. My father had faith like a mustard seed indeed, which God would work on. As for me, I had none of that — it did not make sense at all and when it came to the prayers, I was only going through the motions. The only reason I prayed was because I had been asked to call on heaven. I saw no results in the prayers, because we had no basic needs to begin setting up for the wedding —not even food had been bought.

---

[1] Bride price

Worse still, we had no venue for the wedding. I may not have known what some scriptures really meant at the time; but ***Jeremiah 29:11*** makes good sense to me now*: "For I know the plans I have for you, declares the LORD, plans to prosper you and not to harm you, plans to give you hope and a future."*

By the third week...

Oh, my God! People started trickling to our house with food donations. Many of them got excited after my mother had delivered to them the good tidings that I was getting married. The excitement was so thick that you could slice it with a knife. Our house was now like a warehouse; it was stocked up with food. I saw God's power in all this.

I never imagined people in the neighbourhood would be quite as excited about me getting married. It really puzzled me. *Really! It's me, Chiedza! Why all this happiness? I am not the first one to get married in the neighbourhood, so what's the excitement about?* I wondered. It boggled my mind. I totally forgot we spent a good two weeks praying about it and God was fulfilling our hearts' desires. In fact, my dad's desires — because he came up with the idea.

Then came the million-dollar question: where was the wedding going to take place? I asked my dad and he said, "From church, you are coming home. As you can see, our yard is very big. We can accommodate a lot of people, so your venue is our yard. It's going to be a garden wedding." At that point I felt hot tears streaming down my cheeks. I would never have thought about this even in a million years. How did my dad come up with the idea? He then said, "Your mother and I are going to hire a tent on that particular day."

My aunt, dad's sister, told her friend that her niece was getting married. I was shocked by what my aunt's friend said, "I am going to provide a banner written 'there was a wedding in Canna and Jesus was there'.'" So, the red carpet and the flowers were provided at no charge. It was just unbelievable.

As for the wedding gown, one of my cousins gave me one free of charge. The wedding shoes came from a friend. Her aunt had sent her to sell as part of a business. She also provided the ring-bearing cushions. My hairdo and nails were funded by my sister-in-law. My cousin had bought the weave. I could not believe that I was having a wedding without having to pay for anything. My mother's niece did the video photography for us, again free of charge, while my brother-in-law paid for the photos. *Hooray!*

I was so overwhelmed with all these people willing to help with our wedding as if we had told them, we were penniless. Not forgetting the chairs that we were blessed with — we hired them for free. The only thing we got to buy were the rings. The rest God sent people to help us. That is the Jeremiah 29:11 God!

Whenever I say Jehovah Jireh, I know He is my provider. He provided for me in mysterious ways. After two years, my dad passed away. He had seen my first child as per my request to God. He fulfilled my wishes.

I was crushed and angry with God, however, for robbing me of my prayer partner, the one who prayed that I would have a successful wedding. His death shook me to the very roots of my being and my faith wavered. I struggled to pray. Every moment I thought of praying, I would break down and cry; thinking of my dad and why God had to take him away from me. I had no strength. I would just go to bed without prayer. My husband tried to console me, but I felt that I had been robbed; why my dad? But another voice said, 'But who deserved to die in place of your dad?'

I brushed it off, then one day as I was talking to my mother, I told her that I could no longer pray and all I thought of was my dad. My mother laughed and said, "You're not serious at all! How can you not pray because you miss your dad?" I said to myself, *she does not know the pain I am feeling right now because it is not her dad.* Then she said to me, "You are very privileged you lived with your dad for 31 good years."

Then I responded, "Thirty-one is not much."

Then she said, "How about a child who never saw much of their dad because he died while they were still young?"

Phew! That was an eye opener for me. I had never thought about it along those lines. I beat myself up a bit for not being thankful to God for the 31 good years I spent with my dad.

From that day, I went home and prayed to God. I asked for forgiveness and thanked Him for the time He gave me with my dad. Days went by, and I found myself able to pray again. The healing process started, and I could sing, pray and commune with God again. I picked myself up. Whenever I thought about my dad, it would hurt, but not as much as before my mum had lectured me. I still cry now and again, but the pain is getting lesser day by day. I believe that through prayer, I am getting healed. I thank God for giving me a family and a husband that knows there is God watching over us.

So, prayer is my daily bread. Whenever I need anything that I think might be impossible to get, I challenge myself to pray. I now know that through faith, nothing is too difficult for our God! Do you ever ask? Are there times when you really think God is not there? When problems come, do you ask yourself 'Why me'?

Consider another question: But who? Let's not lose focus on God as we are His children. He will never leave us alone to be devoured by vultures. He created us in His own image and He loves us, but we tend to forget His love because we are busy focusing on our problems and not talking to Him about them. We are called to speak to the mountain, not to speak about the mountain.

Prayer is the master key that unlocks all doors. Never forget to pray, because prayers work; I have experienced the power as you read in my story. They worked for me. Prayer will also work for you. Stay blessed.

5

Navigating Unchartered Territories & Turbulence in **Identity**
Our Mandate to Serve

PAO VIOLA MBEWE

The Esther Crown Analogy
(The Other Side of the Story — Part 1)

Prayer Room – Risen Ladies Retreat

A picture tells a thousand words does sound as cliché. I felt however, it is befitting for me to introduce this chapter with an image that I took at the first Risen Ladies Retreat in 2019.

This image captures a personalised display laid out to create the appropriate, golden-touch and celestial ambience for a sense of cosiness, peace — at rest. We largely operated from the opposite side of this room, but this was the front facing outwards, by the window sill, through which one could view nature and admire the magnificence of God's handiwork — His creation. In this nature was a provision of a sense of tranquillity.

A few years ago, I revisited some instructions the Lord had given to me, to offer a different perspective on varied biblical settings about Leadership and Influence, largely surrounding the female gender and her 'deemed' atypical leadership and management role as perceived in the traditional view of the conventional church, located within the mould of the old covenant.

I had undergone the journey of refining, as the refinery would purify gold, so that in the end, the precious stone is presented with an extreme glow and splendour for its craftsman. One would be presented blameless before the Heavenly Father, having been rescued by the Living Redeemer in Jesus Christ without blemish, looking brilliant and radiant like a purple diamond.

We read the affirmation from God over His presence in such times, that He is sitting by and purifying and purging His children as gold and silver, effectively to bring them into the reflection of HIMSELF. In His righteousness, this is how He achieves the objective — end product perfected, refined. Such continues to be the journey of my life: *"He will sit as a refiner and a purifier of silver; He will purify the sons of Levi, And purge them as gold and silver, That they may offer to the LORD An offering in righteousness..."* **(Malachi 3:3, NKJV).**

The processing of diamonds takes immense pressure for them to be purified to the point where their brilliance is manifested, showcasing the appearance of the precious looking glass with multifaceted angles — square, triangular, circular, oblong, and other such shapes. Yet the most appealing and exhilarating being the diagonal and geometrical polygons — ranging from the Trigon, Quadrilateral or the Quadrangle/Tetragon, Pentagon, Heptagon, Hexagon, Octagon, Nonagon, Decagon, Undecagon; Dodecagon, Icosagon, Pentecontagon and to Hectogon {the latter being 20/ 50/ 100-sided} and so on.

I marvel at the majestic work of the Lord, at the magnificence of His creation. It brings the realisation that God has focused His attention on His creation even more as He mirrors His image.

I was always fascinated by Geometry, such that in high school I would claim every mark on our trickiest and toughest examination papers, to the extent of being intermittently awarded an extra point or two as the teacher would progress with marking the questions that they set to use as a learning point for more effective application in the succeeding lessons past our mock exams.

Two teachers interchanged with Algebra lessons, though we had one main teacher for Geometry. Oft working in synchrony, their tendency was to add one or two questions to a mock exam that would be impossible for the pupils to break through. By God's grace, undoubtedly, I'd decipher these and earn an extra point for 'cracking the code'. On a few occasions in my final year in high school, I earned 101 percent, or 102 percent and the highest at 103 percent for breaking through the impossible geometrical calculations.

Reminiscent of triumphs three decades later, would I say, "Oh, look here I'm smart...?" Simple and straightforward, honest response is — nope! I knew at that early stage, that I had a special dispensation of grace upon my life.

These successes came alongside many a trial, many tears shed each night that I went to bed — when I'd curl up into foetal position — from pain and heartache caused by heartless individuals that made my life unbearable in a boarding high school. I was slandered, my character constantly defamed with no break, my whole being subtly yet progressively assassinated in diabolical acts by some peers who set out to harm me for no apparent reason.

I had to learn to seclude myself to fend off excessive negative impact of their demeanour, I had to acquire strategies that would keep certain personalities at bay so that I tended my little breaking heart. I was one of the youngest three in a class of 50 students. It was tough to keep joy although God created buffers around me that kept me secure in Him. Part of this was relationships that began to emerge through my class performance, as people became aware of my intellect — a few would hang around me for the benefit that would soon trickle down to them. My focus, however, remained towards reliance on the unchanging God, to whom I'd pray in the night before I slept, whose word I realise now that it was His voice. I'd hear as I read up verses that I discovered from the back of my mini-Gideon's Bible — in the 'where to find help' sections. I'd locate verses to address, for instance, "find help when... friends forsake you", in whatever wording the Bible used. I'd read that, and get the desired comfort for my little heart and cry myself to sleep knowing that, though I hurt... God held me close in His loving arms.

So, my classroom performance was some form of sublime and possibly, the only encouragement and comfort I held on to, every three months as I waited for schools to close 'already' — so that I'd go back home, where I was dearly loved.

This happened for the most part of my life from ages 13 to 17, till I went to university where my life changed. I met new people, made new friendships. It was liberating. I found love. It is well, that ends well.

I had God's favour in my home that saw me through as I'd draw out of the same to function when I was at school. I was something special that God viewed with admiration as His own creation. Today, I wonder... as I reminisce over the times of old, and gaze in admiration at these magnificent geometric shapes that I so fell in love with during those high school years...! I reminisce over the life phases during my examinations when I'd meticulously analyse them to precision; so as to derive a correct solution of any question that would be 'tough to crack through'... yet, never baffle me.

And now as I look at the very similar shapes, with added colour and form, the gemstones, in multifaceted precious Jewels and diamonds, mirroring how God would sit and analyse each one of us, that even when exposed to the toughest of life obstacles that would seem most impossible to break through like my Geometrical Challenges, He would focus like my very younger self then invested in delivering the solution by cracking the impossible code. There... as He sits analysing the angles of the trials presenting in my life, HE has to figure it out for me.

I recall, oft during exams, I had to turn the paper upside down or sideways to see the trick that our teachers played in throwing in a deliberate puzzle to an 'angle' — to confuse us, with the intent of eventually teaching us the trick in readiness for national examinations.

Even then, I still managed to *crack the code*. That offered me confidence that in the formation of the Gemstones, it takes Undue review, analysis — therefore investment of time, with precision and affection over the subject (mankind, us) or object (diamond) — to bring out its best. God, the Creator in His role as a Craftsman, has ever been so invested in my life, your life, that He knows how to *crack the code* of the seemingly impossible situations. Inherently, as He sets us apart for a calling, He is fully aware of the abilities He equipped us with, on the preparatory ground set for each of us, enabling us to Soar and impact through our calling. Thus, He is confident when He chooses us to deliver a specific mandate.

The mandate given has each person's name on it — that only they can deliver because He wired them that specific way. Then holistically, we deliver complementarily, to Kingdom business as the B*ody of Christ* with different strengths that make up for Jesus' hands and feet, His mouthpieces. To the glory of the Living God.

We soldier on, navigating the uncharted territory we may find ourselves in. We navigate how to fly through the turbulences as God leads us, through the Deep, above and far beyond familiar Horizons. That's the process through which God takes us, albeit in the refinery. The end product, becoming the unquestionable beauty, of the object, refined heart of man. Stay Positioned! Hallelujah.

Introspection and Embracing a Mandate

All these pieces of precious jewels and gemstones create and exude kaleidoscopic expositions of vibrancy. From my seat, they mirror and reflect the splendour of the King, the glory of the Lord, as is within the aura of an individual that is purified in the Refiner's fire, perfected and qualified, ready to run with God's mission, ready to do His will, God's agenda and not mine, as He releases His mandate over my life and over your life.

I pick the specific image of a gemstone displayed in exhibit 2; as its colour represents Royalty thus a standard in which God holds all whom He created as we acknowledge Jesus as the saviour of the world.

Scripture says we were redeemed out of darkness and brought into God's light, by the birth, death and resurrection of one man in the person of Jesus. We are chosen as a generation that is made HOLY, representing a Royal Priesthood: *"...you are a chosen generation, a royal priesthood, a holy nation, His own special people, that you may proclaim the praises of Him who called you out of darkness into His marvellous light;"* **(1 Peter 2:9, NKJV)**.

It is holy week as I finalise this reflection. Affirming us is that, you and I are presented before the King who is Jesus, as royalty, holy and bought at the price through the shedding of His blood on Calvary — by Jesus Christ.

His role was to bridge a gap to reconcile mankind to the Father after Adam fell short by listening to the enemy, having been influenced to negate God's voice. Jesus paid the separation price by claiming our lives back and restoring them to God once again through His blood shed on the Cross. Leading to His eventual death on Calvary and finally victory was reclaimed by the resurrection. Jesus rose from the dead in three days and that brought salvation to all mankind — the way to reconciling mankind to God — as the original bond had been broken by Eve's reckless action as she was alone, left exposed away from the crucial covering of her husband in the Garden of Eden, as recorded in Genesis 3. How Precious we are to God!

Like a workman who sits for hours on end carving out and mining diamonds in the dark, Jesus's end goal is to cultivate the brilliance of the metal, the stone, from whatever raw material he uses to perfect into, and with its, captivating Beauty and Radiance of that finished product like this diamond presents in you and I.

This Beauty and Radiance in brilliance was only possible because its craftsman invested time and resources to carve it out, remove any unwanted elements, cleanse it of toxicity or intrusive foam like dross that caused impurities to purify it, refine it and release its intrinsic beauty to be presented in its perfect state; that's you and I, holding imputed righteousness before the resurrected King Jesus.

The refining would not be pleasant. As is alluded with most processes of the workmanship in the industry of silversmiths or goldsmiths, perfecting their handiwork — they must patiently work on their pieces and constantly watch them through the burning or melting operation as metal or rock pieces pass through the fire that transforms the raw materials. It is believed that at a melting point, extreme heat and pressure are what cause the brilliance of the diamonds to emerge. This represents you and I in that process of purification and refining; that we are perfect in the eyes that behold us, Christ's view of His creation.

We walk different journeys in life, which teach us to embrace life in different ways based on the path we use to reach our destiny. As the journey continues, we are challenged in the physical or the spirit to trust God beyond question when our faith is tested beyond our ability. Yet that's where God speaks mostly, with certainty if only we attune to the Spirit and hearken to the still small voice. Such have been innumerable intermittent phases of my life.

As I seek God more deeply, to comprehend the extremities of life experiences — the realities of suffering vis a vis seeming flamboyance in my walk, the revelations I get indicate narratives that need unpacking. These would be the times to pause and rethink our positioning — in readiness to reactivating our spiritual senses, which we may be able to discern what God would reveal of the 'hidden' mysteries.

I learn that not all sparkle is flamboyant. Such was the reality to the crown placed on Esther's head. Yet such realities are hidden from ordinary access. What this would mean, I ask. Yet, God reveals hidden things only in the secret place.

I learn that at times this means God taking one out of communion and fellowship with the familiar into a place of seclusion. He allows our isolation from the very close circles — as Jesus did when He went to the solitary place. At times we must walk it alone, without the select few. God may strip us off of the access to our very support system for the raw conversations to happen between Him and us.

These phases of my life release hidden mysteries where I cry out and lose the energy to cry more, then I sob till I can no longer sob. I lay prostrate before the King, totally surrendered to the Father, completely stricken down, on the threshing floor to let go. In letting go, is the letting God and the ultimate and reverent surrender of self — dying to my flesh and allowing Jesus to embody me.

In that is the subduing of my flesh to reflect the embodiment of Christ within me.

In sitting at the feet of Jesus like Mary, and listening to Him, is refreshment and rejuvenation. Mary's story as recorded in

Luke 10:38-39, affirms my posture: *"As Jesus and his disciples were on their way, he came to a village where a woman named Martha opened her home to him. She had a sister called Mary, who sat at the Lord's feet listening to what he said."*

In the Secret Place, I am revitalised in my spirit. I am watered, refilled and refreshed to stand up and dust up, pick myself up after every fall and ready to run with His mandate, not mine, His agenda. Everything about me is stripped off as God's mandate must be released.

Such would be the exhilarating story of the Crown, [to be] placed on one chosen daughter that would run the race with the Kingdom focus. Obedience would take precedence in her assignment.

Everyone wants their position today, but would we all desire her manner of preparation for the crown, the refinery she had to endure. The purification of a Normal to the Noble — would befall one, once a slave girl, one orphan, with the call and mandate to become the queen.

A high price was to be paid over her life, but her focus was solely God's mandate. I've been in such training in recent years. Intense fire and heat rising from all angles. Even as I felt victory is nigh; I could not, could hardly believe, there was yet another battle to fight. Yet God assured me that He trained my hands to war. He is with me and must hold inner peace, the perfect peace that only comes from Him (Isaiah 26.3)

I honour ABBA in His extravagant love. May I not be found wanting when He weighs me on His scale — as I desire to be that diamond or indeed — the precious jewel in any gemstone that was transformed into marvellous light. I honour God for this opportunity to learn and grow in my spiritual walk, blessed to be walking among many spiritual giants and God's generals as I release personal encounters with God.

May ABBA accept the meditation of our hearts and words of our mouths — to bring Him glory in Christ Jesus. We are all called in God's mission, set apart and preserved to serve in different capacities and we must be obedient, embracing the calling within our identity in Christ. He chose us as the ideal option, to lead from our families. Then community impact emerges, beyond that we extend in that trickle-down effect, to towns and cities across the nations and ultimately have global impact.

Simplified views recognise that the family set up is the first port of our call into ministry — to effectively serve our families is delivering God's mandate in learning to equip and empower. In developing future leaders and policy drivers, decision makers of the world to come, we embed the discipline within our family morals and values as we share and implement. We set up the children to be teachable and have receptive attitudes. The teacher is in a calling to educate, and the chef is in a ministry to feed God's people healthy meals etc.

How befitting for our self-reflection within navigation of the uncharted zones on the topic we explore and ponder on. The world view presents a demand that we all must be or consider ourselves the working-class, that means, 'called to serve' in inference from behavioural norms in life as we know it. Yet there are exceptions to the general rule!

The exception acknowledges home-based parents as called to serve their young ones before releasing them into the world — ready with the right survival skills, access to tools, resources and effective strategies to doing life. Mordecai, Queen Esther's uncle, raised her into a successful female that would fit into the palace.

The uncharted Territory, Identity

— Mandate Over Our Lives

This topical discussion centres on a few focal points which will be broadly addressed without specific responses to each point. These only offer us reference points on our exploration:
- How and why the navigation
- How we identify uncharted territory
- Bracing up and positioning for turbulences
- Embracing personal identity
- What's **the Calling**?
- How do we **identify** this **calling vs passion**?
- Where our mandate lies
- Exemplified in Jesus' ministry.

One vital indicator has been, as God calls one to serve in a specific area within spheres, He will not allow them to settle. There will be restlessness within. For as long as I sense a lack of solution to address that area of life within the society that I am linked to, I oblige.

The Revelation

As God releases one for a calling, He has a tendency to remind them, so intensely that they begin to get restless until they can formulate strategies and craft solutions to overcome presenting dysfunctions. As simple and as clear as that!

The calling may represent a passion that causes one so much distress or breaks one's heart — till they devise a solution! In this navigation, I focus on the gender-based review as the uncharted territory. With turbulences being what I consider the challenges one faces.

I refer to this as the preparation on training Ground – to which we can apply biblical theories. I will therefore touch on heroic characters that feature in the Bible.

- ***Deborah the (only) Female Judge*** - What drove her, as God pursued her to restore Israelites?
  I've opted to theme this as **Brokenness to Wholeness** *strategic approach.* Whatever breaks your heart as it does God's - such that you have a burning desire to fix it – and only rest at a solution.

- ***Joanna, the Wife of Chuza*** - King Herod's right hand man's wife. Whatever her burning desire — to share Jesus — she optimised this via access to the palace where her husband served. She impacted in an evangelistic position.
  I opt to theme this **The Opportunistic Approach**. Joanna utilised her position and ministered to Herod's workforce. We hear that she served the Lord with her substance — as the then **one female disciple** of Jesus.

- ***Esther, The Executive Decision* – Direct Call to serve – over her life**
  Esther was directly instructed to serve her people by taking up habitation in the palace in new attire with the affirmation: *"...Yet who knows whether you have come to the kingdom for such a time as this?"* (Esther 4:14b).
  Esther had limited options that would give her relief, let alone her own piece of mind — was she going to compromise her integrity? How would she live with herself should all the Jews be executed according to Haman's genocide plan?
  Unable to allow this to happen, she gave in to Mordecai and took the risk of sacrificing her own life to per-

ish with the Jews should her interception plan backfire. She sends a response to Mordecai with the promise to intervene on the premise that the nation will pray and fast to cover her: *"Go, gather all the Jews who are present in Shushan, and fast for me; neither eat nor drink for three days, night or day. My maids and I will fast likewise. And so I will go to the king, which is against the law; and if I perish, I perish!"* **(Esther 4:16 NKJV)**

The Esther Crown Analogy
The Other Side of the Story – Part 2

Physical Realignment to Mirror Spiritual Positioning
At this mandate, what becomes apparent is that Esther's position and calling to the palace commanded an adjustment to prove 'Fit-for-Purpose'. We will focus on Queen Esther as the key heroine. She must reposition herself and assume a new posture. Her demeanour and stance have changed! She is soon to wear the crown on her noble head. This will require being imminently prepared and militantly armed, for her to take the upcoming office. Here we observe and must recognise that, her calling required a specific and defined level of preparatory work, not only on her part — to be able to get noticed by the king and those surrounding her as waitresses and waiters.

Change was a quest in her functionality and delivery into this 'Divine connection' — into a queen. We see these practical changes taking place in a space of, it is alluded in some research commentaries — six months. What strikes is that her simplistic

life before her mandate, had to be revamped prior to her occupancy into the palace 'as a queen'. The areas in highlight to me include:
- Her Dress Mode – to reflect royalty
- Her Composure – poised, calm, full of grace
- Her Etiquette – conduct of a queenship
- Her Persona – dignity and integrity
- Her Speak – Nobility, Sweet, Soft, Soothing
- Her links – Divine and Kingdom connections
- Her Delivery – Diligence defining her abilities

In all this, Mordecai was Key – this was a typical kingdom Connection beyond their biological link!
The mere presentation of her very self, had to mirror that of a Queen.

She has just shifted positions — from slave girl to queen! Her mannerism must present this reality! Her circle covered her — uncle directing and setting her apart in prayer and the nation praying.

Questions I pondered – what stood out in my spirit?
- Who are the types of circles and network one must yoke selves with?
- What are the biblical characters we can mirror?
- Do these propel us into God's mission or calling?
- How do we maintain spiritual alignment with the vision, not to miss the calling?

To which I then derived the following stages.

Esther's calling to serve – the analysis

First, let's take our positions and thoughtfully unpack the findings of Esther's preparatory journey.

Reflections on world ideologies.

Esther's Identity – given her background, was she qualified to step into the palace? If her calling were deemed appropriate- from whose perspective; how do we perceive this on today's world? Areas to delve into as we reflect:
- How do we perceive her ability within her identity and calling?
- Does God mandate her through the voice of her uncle?

We see that she didn't feel equipped, which presents a humble spirit, yet hers is a direct call from God. She doesn't recognise it. Till she is warned that relief and redemption of the Jews would emerge from elsewhere. Yet she and her father's household would perish. Persuasion from a man who instilled wisdom in her: *"And Mordecai told them to answer Esther: 'Do not think in your heart that you will escape in the king's palace any more than all the other Jews. For if you remain completely silent at this time, relief and deliverance will arise for the Jews from another place, but you and your father's house will perish. Yet who knows whether you have come to the kingdom for such a time as this?'"* **(Esther 4:13-14, NKJV)**

The 'other side of Esther's story' presents the *uncharted territory*, over which Esther lacked familiarity and navigation skills. Till Mordecai stated the consequences and impact of her lack of action to plead for justice she did not fully comprehend her divine calling which would propel her to hold an audience with the king, outside acceptable conditions set by law. There was a risk to her very life.

Identifying SELF as called, in Esther's case, came at a high price. The preceding events would not keep her in a comfort zone. The acceptance and embrace of her mandate, seem as God launching her into action. That knowledge meant her personal agenda had to give. Through Mordecai, she could identify the divine link and hear God's voice.

How she would deliver that mandate depended on further instructions and godly direction? How she would identify appropriate timing — all part of the divine plan that God would execute through her, she had to position herself and oblige.

Our guide for strategic implementation would adopt the *John 5:19* strategy — do as we see the Father do: *"Jesus gave them this answer: 'Very truly I tell you, the Son can do nothing by himself; he can do only what he sees his Father doing, because whatever the Father does the Son also does."* **(NIVUK).**

Did Esther have this option - but her uncle's direction? Scriptural says those led of the Spirit are the sons of God. In the old covenant, we hear Habakkuk's encouragement, over a God-given vision. The analysis continues as we navigate the uncharted zones and reflect on divine direction:

- John 5:19 - Do only as we see the Father do, Spirit-led like Jesus
- Habakkuk 2:1-3- Fullness of time; the vision is yet for the appointed time.
- It may tarry but shall speak.... wait on it!
- Psalm 37:23-24 - for the steps of the righteous are ordered by God: **"The steps of a good man are ordered by the Lord, And He delights in his way.** *Though he falls, he shall not be utterly cast down;* **For the Lord upholds him with His hand.** *I have been young, and now am old; Yet I have not seen the righteous forsaken, Nor his descendants begging bread."*

Divine Positioning and a Call to Action

On a personal level, the highlight within Esther's story is that the unfavourable side does not make the limelight. This would counteract everyone's desire to be the queen. A representation of the turbulences; the emphasis is on the quest to deliver our mandate with spiritual integrity:

- Emulate Christ
- Catch the vision and execute it,
- Walk in obedience to God...
- Catch the season — time is of essence!
- Trust in God's direction without a doubt...

Are we positioned and set apart as fit for purposes — befitting of the calling? This navigation was to consider practical narratives and document the revelations and subsequent lessons to adopt.

The affirmation remains that*: Our mandate reminds us that we are **women** called into ministry – from all directions of the globe. Yet, the operating environment may differ as enablers or deterrents to the level of effectiveness in delivery.*

What does this mean? Challenges surrounding our call include cultural settings and norms. Biblically, we see heroic women who stood out; in the lives of:

1. Deborah the judge
2. Joanna the wife of Chuza
3. **Esther the queen** — faith in action into our servanthood.

The analysis' main focus is directed towards the admirable and anointed women of valour — to use as a benchmark.

In **Deborah**, we see that '*walking the talk*' is not a blissful walk in the park, as reality would present. One commentary biblically holds Deborah in this view, describing her as a true powerhouse: "—mighty combination of judge, intercessor, prophetess, mother of Israel, and military strategist. **Deborah broke outside of her culture—not out of rebellion, but in obedience to God to set her people free.**"

The author of the Deborah anointing edifies her reader and intimates that: "God is calling today's women to a purpose greater than themselves. The Deborah Anointing shows you that although you may have been trapped in tradition and locked into captivity by cultural and gender prejudices, God desires for you to break through these barriers."

Joanna is believed to have held the controversial role of a *Female Disciple* of Jesus, funding His ministry (Luke 8).

As we explore and embrace God's call over our lives in today's culture, we note that experiences and obedience; vis-a-vis world ideologies, may unfavourably impact delivery. As we devise strategies to adopt, it's a call to liberally offer them, to edify, mature and empower us. We are reminded in **1 Corinthians 13:11** that as we shift levels, our communication changes with maturity: *"When I was a child, I spake as a child, I understood as a child, I thought as a child: but when I became a man, I put away childish things."*

May we grow in transparency as we are liberated of the Spirit! Our learning from biblical heroines proves one thing: it is not always a smooth journey.

As we focus on Esther, we see a significant period of time where she gives of self in a marriage to the king, yet neither her heart nor being are in it. She remains there out of obedience to serve a divine calling. Would she have known at this stage, that it was a divine set up?

On reflection, in this day and age, are there similar patterns of persecution and — effectively — 'seemingly abuse' in some settings; and the woman — like Esther remains on hand so as to deliver God's mission... in obliging to a divine calling?

WHAT MANNER OF OBEDIENCE!

Would one equally oblige today? Would this be deemed gender-based violence? The king had access to her intimately, without her 'consent' as we read of her passivity, would this be condemned as a form of violation? What is our perception of this, *viz-a-viz* our true value and self-worth in Christ? Perhaps it is what should hold.

- As we digest this notion; profound reality is the sacrifice of self. Esther's sacrificial offering was her life, to be the martyr for the people.
- What discomfort have we had to endure on the preparatory ground? Esther doesn't appear to notice in the early stages that this was a divine set-up and godly call. She took the risk over a potential tragedy of persecution.
- **Call to action** — may we access the grace to carry real life burdens in our service to the King, into social circles, local communities or others we support in this life.

Led of the Spirit as Sons of God – The Comforter as a Guide in the Triune God.

All in All, we trust that once we are guided of the Holy Spirit, we shall overcome. Romans 8:14 says, "For all those who are led by God's spirit, these are God's sons." We embrace Gods gifts — one of the greatest which is the choice on offer — the privilege of being led by the Spirit of God.

One commentary notes: "As children of God, we can expect to be led by the Holy Spirit which will provide us with the wisdom of God to make the right decisions. Our ability to tap into our calling is much easier when we make decisions based on the leading and guiding of the Holy Spirit. This wisdom will allow us to make decisions today based on knowing what will happen tomorrow. What many people fail to realise is that you can develop a personal relationship with the Holy Spirit just like you already have with God and Jesus."

John 14:26 says, *"But the helper, the Holy Spirit, whom the Father will send in My name, He will teach you all things, and bring to your remembrance all things that I said to you."* The Holy Spirit is not only a personal guide but also a teacher in this life.

Reflective Meditation

In this analysis, I hold one more thought for evaluation in our journey.

Penultimate reflection — in highlighting our navigation alongside obedience to a calling is the position of martyrdom. This enables us to learn and apply to the present challenges that women experience in some settings. I excerpt part of a *Huffpost* observation to edify us: "An orphan raised by her uncle, young Esther was taken against her will as a beautiful virgin to Persian king Ahasuerus's harem. There, she was forced to prepare herself for her first night with the king by spending six months doused in oil of myrrh and another six in sweet odours ointments."

During the night of their union, Ahasuerus loved Esther "above all women" and made her the Persian Empire's Queen. Esther replaced Queen Vashti, who had been sentenced to death because she had refused to obey the King's commandment to dance in the nude for his guests during a feast.

The Talmud reveals that Esther's relationship with Ahasuerus wasn't a romantic one. Esther remained passive and allowed the king to rape her repeatedly. Esther despaired throughout her first six years in the palace. She remained passive and obedient to the moody king.

Retrospection

How can we explain Esther's abrupt change in behaviour from deep despair to determined action and from passiveness to leadership? Hearing the horror of the planned genocide, the light went on: Esther connected with her inner self and understood why she had been made queen.

She understood why she had to suffer through her relationship with this irritable king. She understood that she had a mission and that she could shape reality rather than passively suffer through it. Esther had been made queen to save her people; her mission and her faith shaped her character and inspired her to act and succeed.

After the immediate danger to her community passed, Queen Esther stayed with Ahasuerus. Why did she stay with him, rather than restart her life? We need to put the book of Esther into an historical context to better understand Esther's choice. The story of Esther happened after Cyrus, the first Persian king, called for all deported Jews to return to Jerusalem to build the House of God (538 B.C., Ezra 1:2).

Most of the Jews preferred the comfortable life of the Persian Empire to an arduous life rebuilding their devastated homeland. The Talmud sees Haman's decree as a punishment from Heaven to these Jews.

When, several years later, Nehemiah asked the Persian king for permission to return to Zion and rebuild Jerusalem, *"the queen is seating by him"* **(Nehemiah 2:6)**, and she influenced the king's decision to approve Nehemiah's request.

The Queen described in the book of Nehemiah is Queen Esther. She stayed with Ahasuerus and sacrificed her personal happiness to complete her ultimate mission to enable the building of the Second Temple and the return to Zion.

Navigation Relevance and the Mandate

- What can we learn from Esther about our personal understanding of our true life's mission? Do you, or does someone you know, demonstrate the same total commitment to a mission, even at the cost of sacrificing personal happiness?
- Finally, herewith the popular conflict that may at times deter our service — how do we overcome — in practical terms as we apply biblical truth as per God's word. How do we deal with the complexity of the marriage submission and the 'unsaved or uncalled' husband? *"Wives, submit to your own husbands, as to the Lord. For the husband is head of the wife, as also Christ is head of the church; and He is the Saviour of the body. Therefore, just as the church is subject to Christ, so let the wives be to their own husbands in everything."* **(Ephesians 5: 22-24).**

Observation: It appears that the latter part of this verse may not be adequately emphasised in some settings e.g., largely, in the so-called emerging economies: **Husbands, love your wives, just as Christ also loved the church and gave Himself for her,** that He might — sanctify and cleanse her with the washing of water by the word, that He might present her to Himself a glorious church— holy and without blemish. So, husbands ought to love their own wives as their own bodies; he who loves his wife loves himself. For no one ever hated his own flesh, but nourishes and cherishes it, just as the Lord does the church. For we are members of His body, [h] **of His flesh and of His bones**. "For man shall leave his father and mother and be joined to his wife, and the two shall become one flesh." This is a great mystery, let each one of you in particular so love his own wife as himself, and let the wife see that she respects her husband. (Excerpt: vs 24-33).

Questions to Consider
How does one effectively engage, should the husband not take counsel from the Lord? Maybe these are areas we may explore in the next volume. May we remain anchored in the Triune God.

Prayerful Inspiration
Through this exploration, may His will prevail as we oblige to His calling.

May God edify us in, alerting our spirit man to operate from His view.

May we seize every opportunity to learn, as God orders our steps as God's righteousness.

Every spiritual blessing to each reader and partakers of the grace, the chosen of the many called.

Thanking the Lord for rich blessings and direction in this learning. It is humbling to know that God sees us each worth of His calling. Yet we must stand positioned and in alignment.

In reverent surrender lies the preparatory ground so that we are set apart, purified as vessels of honour. As the precious stones and jewels that God perceives us to be.

May we stand ready and willing as *'Team Jesus'* - with an unending love and commitment to delivering the heart of God across the nations.

As we honour each of God's vessels, as we bless Him for their endearing service.

That the nations hearken to the voice of the Lord because they said 'yes' to the calling.

We are empowered as we observe from the distance and tap in graces — while we sit under Generals of the Most-High God – to tap in on their mentorship abilities.

We pray that we all shall soon catch the mantles that await, and run with God's vision, in due season.

As for me, I still unpack much of the knowledge and revelations in the journey of obedience. For now... it's Shalom Saints. Remain highly favoured of the Lord. Glory to the King of Kings. Hallelujah to the Lord of Hosts.

My All, for His Glory...

References:
1. Six Ways to Know God's Calling for you.
2. The Tragic Life of Queen Esther.

Image Credits: https://www.crystalinks.com/purplediamond.jpg

6

Grace And Mercy Abound &
Renew
The Journey through Loss, Grief and Mourning

NUNUDZAI S. T. NGORORO

Dedication

To the phenomenal men who taught me 'much' in the 'university' of my life: **Simeon John Ngorora,** *my late father, was my first warrior, defender, promoter, protector, disruptor... who passed away, suddenly on 22.04.2004. My name was safe in his mouth.*
John Rosmond Imbeah, *my late husband, who passed away in a car crash on 02.04.2015.*

An avalanche of trauma and stress drew in, over a period of, altogether 16 adventurous and turbulent years.

John Brian Runyararo Chikombero *was like my twin — my cousin, my brother as a perfect partner — my friend, my safe go-to person, my biggest fan, who died of COVID-19 on 21.01.2021, my world felt cruel, as I never got a chance to say 'goodbye'.*

This write up is in memory of my family members.

Great is your MERCY toward me, Your loving kindness towards me, Your tender mercies I see day after day, Great is your GRACE... forever faithful towards me, you always provide for me. — **Donnie McClurkin**

THE very centre, the core, of the Bible, is the Gospel. It is the fundamental expression and teaching of the Grace and Mercy of God, which is the 'too-good-to-be-true' news. This is the most important concept in the world. It is expressed in the unfailing promises of God's love, revealed in scripture and embodied in Jesus Christ, bringing us forgiveness of sin. All we need to do is to believe it in our hearts and receive it by faith.

This activates tangible benefits of emotional and mental healing, wisdom, prosperity and many treats all wrapped up in a huge present — an inclusively packaged gift or deal called salvation, which encompasses atonement for sin. Grace and Mercy speak to the reckless, would-be-considered 'scandalous' great exchange between a holy God and sinful men. It is love demonstrated to the unlovable, peace given to the restless, unmerited favour to an underserving and dying world, prosperity to the poor, healing for the sick and freedom for the oppressed.

Grace and Mercy are expressions of pure, unadulterated love that gets inconvenienced, stops to care, stoops down to rescue, unconditionally reaches downwards to a rebellious and ill-deserving people 'kicking against' the Maker. Grace and Mercy are most needed and best understood in the midst of sin, the separation from love, in suffering, and brokenness. That is why everyone needs Grace and Mercy to live well. Grace and Mercy are not *karma*, which is all about getting what you deserve. Grace and Mercy are incredible for you get what you do not deserve, and you do NOT get what you do deserve.

God Himself provides Grace and Mercy so that anyone in need of forgiveness or acceptance is offered LIFE in abundance. Grace and Mercy are never about us and what we do. Grace and Mercy have always been about God: His own uncoerced initiative, pervasive, extravagant demonstration of His reckless love, care, and favour for us — from the beginning of time and that has never changed. In Grace and Mercy, God freely gives us, intimate relationship with Himself — His nature, which is faithful, goodness, love, provision, and healing that is Jesus Christ. God Himself is in redeeming action for us.

We live victoriously every day by accepting the gift of the Grace and Mercy of God, which are already provided for us. It is the basis for our true identity, worth, significance and security — Grace and Mercy! I thank you that today I can do life with You, Lord, every moment and every day of my life.

I was a sinner. But God knew that; He took my sin from me, so I could be made right with Him. There is no more quarrel between God and I because of the Lord Jesus Christ. (2 Corinthians 5:21). My worth is priceless.

I lose my way on occasion, but God knows that; He gave His Spirit to live in me, guide me, enable and empower me (1 Corinthians 6:19, John 16:13, Acts 1:8). Through GOD, by the Holy Spirit, my significance is intact.

I need a second chance, more chances… But God knows that, so He provided me with a way back to relationship with people, through confession and repentance (according to 1 John 1:9, Luke 24:47). Through God, my security is entrenched.

The trinity and infinity are impossibly notorious — a love none can define or compute. Jesus shows us what it means to be merciful: a relationship based on forgiveness and love, reconciliation and truth. An intimate relationship with the Godhead displays the unmistakable face of God's Grace and Mercy.

Against this backdrop, may the GRACE of our Lord Jesus Christ, the LOVE of God our Father and the sweet FELLOWSHIP of the Holy Spirit be with you and your family and all your relationships as you continue reading!

***

On April 2, 2015, my husband John, who was Ghanaian, died on the spot on the highway in a fatal car crash. I did not cry at the funeral. I performed. Akin to a woman in labour, I keened; from somewhere deep inside came a guttural howling sound. Real tears would not come for the following two agonising years. The moment those bosses from work walked into my lounge that fateful morning, my heart and mind immediately froze. Short-circuited. Overloaded. I thought that I had lost my mind there and then. I describe it like a collision impact, where the fragments of the windscreen of a vehicle do not spill over, but the shattered glass of my heart and mind were kept in place, held, and jelled by Grace and Mercy's infinite wisdom. Over time Grace and Mercy then began a very slow process of fixing each broken piece one by one. Defragmentation. I am loading…

From the beginning of that fateful year, unbeknown to me, I had already begun to grieve. There was inexplicable foreboding, a heaviness that I just simply could not shake off. My vitals, my blood pressure and blood sugar were perfectly fine, as they still are today. As a couple, my husband and I experienced an amazingly difficult, interesting, and troubled marriage. We would never have made the couple of the year in any given period. Grace and Mercy restrained us from being too unkind and cruel to each other. We were clueless as to how to do marriage properly.

As is the reality of life, there are no universities to study for 'husbanding' or 'wifing'. No educational curriculum the world over is designed to equip people for the most important of jobs, spousal and parental assignments. Something is very wrong with that picture. Since my husband had been married before, I naturally assumed that he would know how to make the marriage a success. It never ever crossed my mind that marriage is spelt '*W-O-R-K and F-O-R-G-I-V-E-N-E-S-S*'.

A divorcee comes from a break-up and break down of a marriage in his repertoire, the shattering of covenant. That is a huge red flag. A bride usually just wants to get married, have a wedding, never mind the ever after.

There definitely were times we disagreed extensively, when I wished we could part ways, but that Easter morning, no matter what our differences, I did not want him dead. Yet he was and there was nothing, absolutely nothing, I could do about it. He was dead, without question — as one would hope in disbelief... and that set me off course!

I must have been in a *'crab frying'* mood. In retrospect, there was white hot burning anger that I carried with me. I did not have the remotest idea, as to where to put it down, where to bury it. What was beneath that anger? More anger. What was beneath that? Even more anger. And beneath that? Fear. Irrationality. Misdirected and unanswered questions, petrifying pictures of dysfunction and distortion of life, a future without my husband!

Fear can destroy; it can kill someone in distress, and debilitate you. Fear is not a friend. I felt super mad at John for driving late at night. His eyesight was not great. Moreover, he was an 'early night' type of person. It was out of character to drive such a long distance on an unfamiliar road. Zimbabwe's roads are mostly car unworthy. I was furious at him for having too much faith in the safety record of his huge car. He drove an ML430.

I was upset at John for sending that awful WhatsApp message to everyone in his contact list, "Today I'm going to tell my wife, that like Jesus, I'm going to disappear for three days and resurface again on Sunday." Oh, he came back on Sunday all right: in a coffin! Warren Hills Cemetery became his permanent address. This is the level of anger and pain that I suffered!

I was livid— at God. How? Why? When? Where? What? And then...? I had prayed for my husband, our four sons, fasted, cried, and pleaded for our marriage. Not this! Me! In my assessment — it was too tragic, what had happened to ME. Not fair!

Yet more drama was to unfold that year, culminating in a nasty nervous breakdown. The verdict: my heart and my mind were too broken. But Grace and Mercy patiently, relentlessly, pursued me. It is no lie that the Grace and Mercy of God will not tear down to set you free, and makes a way for you to come out of any situation. It is important to cooperate and wait UPON this Grace and Mercy, and in Grace and Mercy. Self-aware. Self-confident. Self- assured in the Grace and Mercy. Because self-centred, self–loving pride, produces unreasonable anger and grief; leading us into crisis after crisis and chaotic lives — which I think is what I went through.

My husband died away from our city. They required a next of kin to go and authorise collection and release of the body from Kwekwe. I categorically refused. I also did not want the body at the house. I do not know why we must put the coffin in the house at all, as though there are no funeral parlours. The elders were horrified at the untraditional, uncouth, cavalier decisions that I was making. But I had my reasons, which they would not understand.

The funeral parlour was a few minutes away from our home, but for the three days that he lay there, I would not go near his body. They tried to force me to go. How dare he come all the way from Ghana to Zimbabwe, marry me, die and leave me alone with the boys? Just like that! Who does that? He never even took out funeral insurance. He insisted that it was a waste of money. His plan was to return to Ghana, retire there, and die among his people. He always vehemently swore that he would not die young. Ever so careful with his diet, exercise, health, his security, his safety and coming from a family line of longevity, that clocked the centennials.

The morning of the burial on April 6, 2015, I delayed and delayed. My brother knew that I was not going to the parlour. No one else did. I locked myself in my bedroom with a friend. In my book, it was not a 'crime' if I didn't attend. What was left of my husband, in my view, was just the shell, the corpse, the body. We do not even refer to it by name. It is the body, the corpse, *chitunha*, icy cold for that matter, from the freezer. I hate being cold.

I longed for my mum. She would have understood. She had a pre-booked to fly to New Zealand and left the eve of the burial for a four-month visit to my younger sister. She was so conflicted. Her staying would not 'raise' John from the dead. I did not wish for my mother to go away, but I had to release her. Historically, on April 18, 1980, Sally Hayfron Mugabe, stood alone in a foreign land, as her husband was being sworn in as independent Zimbabwe's first Prime Minister. Back home, in Ghana, on the same day, Sally's mother and grandmother and siblings missed her at the burial of her father. John's grandfather... *It is life... Or rather, it is death.*

I finally saw the white coffin draped in royal *kente* cloth. John loved white. I wonder why we cover the coffin at all, though. There it was, set in front of the huge indoor basketball auditorium, the 1500-plus crowd, seated. It was a public holiday. Easter. Where had ALL these people come from? The funeral proceedings were boring. Long speeches. I could not, would not, stay still. On so many occasions and functions I had sat in that auditorium, with John. I did not want to be there. My brother, sitting next to me, made a pact with me and bribed me that as long as he massaged my neck, I was not allowed to move, nor permitted to talk. I agreed. I absolutely love hugs and massages. The one thing I did like about that weekend, were the hugs. Fat ones, thin ones, scented ones, sweaty smelly ones, male ones, female ones, long ones, short ones, hard ones, soft ones, old ones, young ones!

Zimbabweans are not very touchy or cuddly except at funerals. That was so awesome, comforting. When I eventually went back to work, Grace and Mercy followed me there. Each day the principal, not a hugger by nature, would open out her arms and hug me and say, "How are you today? Come, I know you like hugs."

Body viewing could not be avoided. A crowd stormed me. People who had not made it to the house before then, took a chance to show their sympathy, pay condolences, right there. It was military and presidential guard style; my brother marshalled personnel and created a shield to block off highly offended friends and relatives. The funeral director was waiting upon me. We did not have the whole day. John lay there, as though nothing was missing or broken. Permanently silent. *Benya John Rosmond Imbeah, 55 years old*. Healthy. Fit. Gone... Just like that!

The whirlwind beneath my wings, against which I had to rise — I did not cry, trying to compute it all. I had seen thousands of similar scenes. I just never imagined that it would be me. The lady funeral attendant would not let me touch him, kiss his forehead, his eyes. Forbidden. Something about dangerous chemicals. I had kissed my dad, though. My father's body had been shockingly freezing cold, from the mortuary, of course. I had never ever touched a dead body prior to that. He, too, passed on in the month of April in 2004. April 22. He was called John, too. What was it with these Johns leaving me? John, my dear darling cousin slipped away on January 21, 2021. COVID-19 stinking rules, no body, no funeral rites, no attendance. Just the awful pain of loss, grief, mourning.

Back to John's funeral — with my uncle on my left, my brother-in-law on my right, I was escorted to the car for the cemetery.

On April 6, we left him at Warren Hills Cemetery, alone in the dirt, in the dark. He hated both. How awful! Mud. Worms. Bacteria. Decomposition. Two days later, I had to be in Kwekwe, to collect the death certificate and, deal with the car, that ML430. I auctioned her — I had to. *Pronto!*

Then, on April 15, Jillian, my amazing witty intelligent friend and colleague, with whom I had been together since high school — in the hockey, tennis Teams and French teaching and culture world in Zimbabwe — died!

Five days later, *nyaradzo,* as a memorial service is referred to in Shona, was held for John. This time, Grace and Mercy and I pulled off a celebratory Ghana-Zimbabwe affair, with a singing creative arts devotional. A tribute to the man who had actually said, "I do". He had spent the rest of his life in my nation, with me and gave me four sons. Today he lies in Zimbabwean soil, on the other side of Heroes Acre, where his other mother, Sally Mugabe, lies…

On July 7, 2015, John's mother died in Ghana. Memaa, born on July 18, and I, born on July 21. John usually called her and we would wish each other birthday greetings. That year was different. Silence. John was no more. Memaa was no more.

On July 8, Irina, my extraordinary creative Yugoslav artist friend, died. Our last project together was John's amazing huge memorial scrap book, branded mementos, thank you cards and journals — appreciation tokens.

To top it all up, on September 31, 2015, I was unexpectedly retrenched from my job at a Christian international school. While these things happened — it was just that at that particular time it most certainly was not welcome news. Too soon. Another big loss. That was why it stung so hard. A rug seemed to have been pulled from under me.

In a space of five months, the onslaught of multiple big losses began to take its toll. Home was too lonely, suddenly too large, too quiet, awfully scary, just myself and my two younger boys, 13 and nine years respectively at the time. As a mover and shaker, I half-heartedly convinced myself that I could sort all the mess out. What bothered me was that I could not sleep for days on end, thus I drank red wine.

It helped a little. I needed more and more to feel somewhat better. Still, I could not sleep. I desperately longed to sleep. My head buzzed; too much nervous energy. I was hyperactive. It was exhausting. I was a nuisance. I could not think nor process the gazillion questions. Inadequate one-dollar answers to multimillion dollar queries and "what ifs" were crushing in. I began to crash, to black out. Still, I could not sleep. The insomnia was nasty, unresponsive even to sleeping pills. Days and nights merged into a blur. My mind took a life of its own. I could not shut my mind down. Thousands of negative thoughts collided each day. I was scared, confused, foolish, reckless, demanding, and stubborn. I longed to sleep... forever. People who commit suicide do not want to die. They just want the pain to stop.

Love is lived from the heart. My heart was broken and frozen. Decisions are made from the mind. My mind was a spaghetti bowl, labyrinth of disorganised chaos. Never having been ordinarily laser-focused, single-minded, or rigidly-structured, in my outlook, I spiralled fast... down a dark abyss.

Finally, in October 2015, Grace and Mercy came in the form of my best friend, who flew in from France to spend time with me. She began to raise the alarm. It was not an exaggeration. She persisted. She knew the warning signs. Danger ahead. She increased the distress, anywhere, everywhere, including to our psychiatrist friend.

On August 6, 2016, we had a Baby Welcome ceremony for my niece. Patriarchal ownership of our first. The hype. The anti-climax went on... Something was wrong.

Further, on April 8, 2016, we had my mother's 70th birthday luncheon festivity. It was extremely stressful. I juggled too many balls and dropped a big one on the day. Exhaustion set in. The cracks were widening. The silent warning screams began to increase in volume and intensity. Irritations surfaced; so did my disappointments.

I ended up with a situation on June 12, 2016. Drunk. I flew into a rage at my niece's first birthday party. Our only brother's first child, my heiress. I got into an argument with my uncle. It was adversarial and vitriolic. In her bid to restrain me from the back, I lashed out and physically struck my mum. Culturally, it is the ultimate crime.

Three days later, totally drunk; I crashed my car on campus. Grace and Mercy fully stepped in! While Evil tried to stop redemption, Grace and Mercy said "No".

Darkness tried to steal my heart. Life and death stood face to face with me. Justice demanded punishment. Grace and Mercy said no. They would not let me go. Sin was not allowed to take me over. When I could not keep myself together; Grace and Mercy became my keepers. The net closed in. The choice to self-destruct was taken from me.

At this point, my brother took guardianship of the boys. The specialist psychiatrist interned me into a hospice: chronic maniac depression/bipolar, cognitive dissonance, were all undergirded by compounded sorrow and grief... it seemed? What animal was that this maniac depression/bipolar? This pervasive, punishing, tormenting thing had a name! My tormented soul, mind, will, emotions and heart put me into a mould that I desperately wanted to break out of and escape from. A spiritual dilemma. Mental health and Depression... With no feasible solution.

A chronic affective disorder. Medication for life. I did not agree. Sadly, at the time, I had no alternative to proffer. Stuck! Few really understood, wanted to, or attempted to. It was way too scary. See, a disease needs physical evidence like boils, skin rash, broken limb, or a swollen something for people to believe. There was none. This crazy thing that I was experiencing, and manifesting became a phenomenon. It was somewhat incompatible with the faith. I was failing dismally. This side of heaven, terrible things do happen to good people.

Mistakes were made. A broken heart and a tormented mind seem strange, so threatening, so unreal, a source of shame. Even the courts of the land protect mental health sufferers. Hosea 4:6 says, "My people perish for lack of knowledge."

So many aspersions, acts of communicating false statements. People can be so careless, so cruel, so unkind, so fearful, so ignorant. Too much damaging slander, whispers behind my back. It did not hurt at all, until it was being done by the insensitive, ignorant, hurtful... in my children's hearing. I bled for my sons, conjuring up visions of their mum on the streets picking rubbish out of bins, sleeping out, wandering, half-naked, dirty, lost.

The boys were terrified.

Our town house simply became the "flat". The door was closed shut, locked, for three years. I did not think to drape the furniture. A home is just but a house if no one lives there. The boys and I lived out of three homes: at my brother's and my sister's, among their families, their accommodating spouses and my mum's home in two cities. I will never know what it cost them. Grace and Mercy had extended to us, inconveniences suffered on our behalf, especially gracious were my in-laws. I am just ever so grateful that the boys and I had a safety net.

My siblings had no legal filial obligation to look after us, but they did. My mother too, clucked, and fussed. Grace and Mercy in action. We moved the boys' bedroom, wholesale, to my sister's home. Losses. Changes. Grief. Frustration. Downsizing. Adjustments. The boys had to be transferred from their international Christian day school into local boarding school. I was unable to care for them daily. My little one hated boarding school with a passion. After a year, he got so ill that the paediatrician's team were stumped. He had developed psychosomatic illness, unable to keep any food down and just became as skin on bones.

We already intuitively know that we are separated from God and in need of saving and rescuing. There is, therefore, no need to take an approach that condemns — we already feel condemned. What we need is the Grace and Mercy, the *too good to be true* news, the full Gospel – that empowers people to receive the forgiveness of their sins, the healing of their bodies, the deliverance from oppression, suppression, dysfunctional relationship and whatever else we need.

Unseen barriers exist which have taught me that judging a desperate person buying alcohol or cigarettes is folly. The nights are cold, the world unfriendly, everything is painfully uncomfortable. You suffer injuries or chronic conditions that bother you with little or no access to medical care and not much healthy food. In that uncomfortable, over-stimulating context, needing a drink or some cigarettes makes sense, to warm up and get to sleep. With under-nourishment, a few smokes may be the only thing that kills the hunger pangs, so that you can survive. People who have never been stressed, tormented or burdened to the point of blacking out do not think this way. They want to moralise the decisions of abused women, mentally ill, poor people, prostitutes, homeless, perhaps to comfort themselves about the injustices of the world, rather than acknowledging the situational factors and reaching out in love. When you do not fully understand a person's context, it is easy to impose abstract, rigid expectations on them.

The demand is that disenfranchised people must do better. They are already doing the best they can. If a person's behaviour does not make sense to you, it is because you are missing a part of their context. It is through the Grace and Mercy lens that we need to look for what we have mistaken as signs of failure — there is no failure that Grace and Mercy cannot have compassion for, empathise with and salvage.

People hurt badly; they have deep issues and needs. The more we embrace the lost and lonely and offer Grace and Mercy, the more we can help people thrive. Selfish unloving people remain judgmental, against those with mental illness; depression is interpreted as laziness, mood swings are framed as manipulative people with "severe" mental illnesses are assumed incompetent or dangerous. In an environment where Grace and Mercy recognise legitimate barriers, sufferers thrive and heal in the presence and atmosphere of pure unconditional love. With rejection we flounder. We feel shame about our assault histories, our anxiety symptoms, and our depressive episodes.

If a person cannot get out of bed, something is making them exhausted. If a person is not doing life well, even if a person is actively choosing to self-sabotage, there is a reason for it. People do not wilfully choose to fail or disappoint. No one wants to feel incapable, useless, stupid, idiotic, apathetic, or ineffective. Let us pay more attention and not judge by offering Grace and Mercy. Perfect love drives out all fear. Lover never fails.

I could not defend myself. I gave up even trying to explain anything. My behaviour was deemed incompatible with a strong, capable, professional, super smart, super intelligent woman. Well, here we were! Mercy held my mind together. Grace allowed me to understand the warfare; that I was in a battle for my life. Debilitating depression crushes the mind, soul, emotions, locks a person and knocks them down, intending to take them out. It is demonic suppression and oppression. I did not talk, read, write, sing, laugh, cry, dance nor play. I could and would not cook, so I did not break bread or have any true fellowship with anyone. I could and would not pray, so petitions in the courts of heaven were not submitted. I could and would not laugh, so windows to the soul closed the blinds. Submarine, I dived to the seabed and stayed there, once a while torpedoing a friend, a family member or two, surfacing for just a little while but mostly retreating to the cold dark depths.

From midway into 2016 to the end of 2018, I was in a space and place ever so far away. I did not know how to find my way back to sanity. I worked some, but I did not job. I switched off my phone. I would not answer it if it flashed. Dropped out of social media groups. Lost contacts. Grief-share meetings of widows talking of their beloved loving husband upset me. I wanted to move on. I was stuck.

In 2017, Dr. Renner, Ghanaian urologist, dies; John's uncle who adopted Zimbabwe at independence as his home. He signed the marriage certificate for us on behalf of John's family. I was not informed. I learnt it by chance. Loss, grief, mourning, loss, and more loss.

Medication numbed my brain. My mum, a retired nurse, was my 24-hour carer. Grace and Mercy as family and friends rallied. Provision for boys and I. I was emotionally, intellectually, spiritually, psychologically, physically, socially unavailable to anyone, especially to my boys. Self-centred. Disconnected. I knew that, negative horrible thoughts were just so awful but I did not know how to fix myself. After sleepless days, super exhaustion would set in. Now I appreciate why POW, prisoners of war, are deprived sleep as a torture method. I was a walking dead person. Sometimes I just stayed in bed, for days at a time. I had forgotten, though, that I still had books unpublished, a bigger classroom to teach, my nation, heads of state to mentor. I had forgotten that intellectual integrity, moral authority, transforming moulding future leaders, creating life, laughter, and love was my mandate. I had forgotten that there were broken silent men who needed a safe and sane space and place to express themselves.

Church became rather irrelevant. Somehow my experience, did not match with the Grace and Mercy's gift of freedom, liberty, joy, comfort. I was unhappy, running to sanity, to safety, but this legalistic religious wall, impenetrable, fixed, ridiculous, an impasse was not useful. Church felt stale. Prayer and study and fellowship were a chore. Scripture bounced off me and could not, would not, take root nor grow fruit. My heart was cold, frozen, and impenetrable. In any case, a young widow becomes a strange "status". You are neither single nor married, a pariah, a threat to married women. A sport for married men. By default, fellowship programs exclude you. Grace and Mercy fuss about being the husband of the widows and the father of the fatherless, the orphans. I could not compute it, the exclusion, incongruence, hostility, ignorance. I stayed away.

On December 31 2016, Grace and Mercy smiled on us. Kobina, our eldest son's wedding to Maria, a Zimbabwean gazelle. His mother was unable to attend from Ghana. I was asked to stand in as the mother. An honour. I inherited him, a skinny, scrawny and scraggy pimply thin, angry teenager at my marriage, only 15, turned warrior, defender, protector, soldier, nurturer... husband. I was anxious. If only John was still there? John's older brother, the formidable chief, Nana Nanabanyin Ninsin-Imbeah, came. A gracious pleasure. A covering.

Sometime between 2016 and 2018. Losses. Changes. Grief. Frustration. Downsizing. Losses. Adjustment. Downsizing. Losses. So, life had turned inside out and upside down.

I missed a big part of me. Winters were painful. The realisation that I would never ever again, be with this tall gentleman at 6 feet, one who provided love and warmth by my side, broke my heart. The absence of the person who now left; an imagination of them lying away in their resting place forever, was hard to think of. I missed a big piece of me, my heart, and my mind, worried that I had lost it forever. What the real "it" was, I could not quite explain. I missed many small familiar things, even the squabbles. I had figured that in my husband, I had finally found my very own person to annoy for the rest of my life. John and I were squabbling siblings. I do not remember much of what we fought about. We did not fully understand the purpose of marriage. There is so much I needed to say and to do differently. It was way too late. I could definitely have been kinder over the 16 years that I knew him.

On April 16 2018, Grace and Mercy showed up in full force that morning, penetrating my heart, flooding it with love, hugging me in a warm embrace of compassion. Matthew 11: 28-30

MSG: "Are you tired? Worn out? Burned out on religion? Come to me. Get away with me and you'll recover your life. I'll show you how to take a real rest. Walk with me and work with me—watch how I do it. Learn the unforced rhythms of grace. I won't lay anything heavy or ill-fitting on you. Keep company with me and you'll learn to live freely and lightly."

I wept. Deep sobs from within, for hours that morning, a dam burst. It was cathartic. Three years of punishing the body, not eating well or exercising, tension, stress, insomnia, I developed a permanent frown. I had greyed almost overnight. Memories, sadness, loss, grief, bittersweet sadness, happiness, safe. My father's house was a safe and sane space and place. Rediscovering, light, colour, beauty, scented oils, preparing food with my boys, doing chores for the boys, with love and great joy was healing. Laughing, jogging, shopping, going to church, hosting sleep overs, playing cricket, planning, squabbling, bantering, going for walks with them... in my town of origin, telling them stories, escapades, going back in time, a happier, less chaotic time.

I sobbed on the bathroom floor as huge weight slipped off my shoulders. I felt awfully vulnerable but so very safe. I had come to the end of myself. This was new, strange, but welcome. I had missed my tears. The prolonged, stubborn selfish locked up grief is punitive. It makes you ill. It finally disengaged and changed gears into mourning cruise. Blessed are those who mourn. Mourning is beautiful, a gift, remembering, grateful, comforting. Slowly, incrementally, kaizen, allowing Grace and Mercy the problem solver to work. It can do exceeding, abundantly above all I could ever think or imagine. I may have expected certain outcomes, my way, but Grace and Mercy's way is far better than my way.

Peace has found a home, from knowing that Grace and Mercy are awesome in this place, right here, right now where I am, no matter the circumstances outside and around me. I have embraced life skills, a lifestyle for life care, in my lifetime and to pass on generationally. I am going to fly again, higher, when I am truly back on my feet again. I am experiencing the golden sunrise and sunset. I am awake. I had missed the sun and the Son. They did not go anywhere. I am weeping everywhere, anywhere, tears just roll down, as the heart is thawing, tender again. I am in love again with people.

With everything, including my crazy special nation. I have rediscovered my voice, my agency. Grace and Mercy has enrolled me however in the class for patience, humility, and true love. Years of atrophy cannot be righted in a jiffy. When scripture bounced and Jesus seemed unreal, when medication was too slow and side effects unpleasant, when almost nothing made sense or was purposeful. I was lost. Who do you cling to? Who do you go to? What can you do? When life turns inside out and upside down and bubbles bursting any which way? What do you do? The complexities of when loving hurts and yet you do not know why compound grief. My marriage hurt a lot and I did not know why. When multiple tragedies occur and the losses overwhelm you... Where do you go? What do you do? Unfortunately, there is no quick relief for grief matters for the restless, the impatient, the angry, the unforgiving.

Life is understood backwards but must be lived forward. — Soren Kirkergard

Grace and Mercy has been there in the past, present, future and will never leave me.

It has broken down barriers, torn down lies and scaled walls to rescue me. It finally dawned on me that Grace and Mercy are not responsible of the bad things that happen to good people this side of heaven. Sin is. The thief comes to steal, kill and destroy. God is good, always. He is not guilty.

Grace and Mercy went before me, around me, besides me, all around me, so loved and cherished me always, even when I thought otherwise. God's hands, heart, feet and pockets in action appeared through many people. Incredible acts of kindness, countless number of prayers across the continents. Grace and Mercy fought for me when I had lost the plot and was ready to give up. Relationship is paramount. Forgiveness takes one person and that one person is you. Reconciliation takes two or more people and cooperation from the parties involved. Rebuilding the broken bridges takes a long time, sometimes a lifetime. It requires, work, effort, time, resources, to mend, messed up relations.

Hurting People hurt other People.

My exhortation is this, hang in there, dear friend! one day at a time, one hour at a time, one moment at a time There is nothing that happens to you, no temptation known to anyone, that has never happened before, but God makes a triumphant way thorough it for us. Your faith, identity, security, cannot be in your marriage, your children, yourself, your degrees, your connections, your money, your nationality, but in God the Almighty Father, the creator of the universe. The greatest problem we have is the one prideful thought and attempt to do life on our own, to be our own God, missing the whole purpose of Grace and Mercy is to make life easy. We are not smart enough to run our own lives.

Love. Live. Laugh. Learn. Love. Live. Laugh. Learn. Love. Live. Laugh. Learn. Love. Live. Laugh. Learn. Love. Live. Laugh. Learn.

7
From
Trauma to Transformation
My Story, Your Story, Our Story
If Only I Knew then What I Know Now...

GLAD BARTRAM

THERE is no pain that God cannot use for something good, but if only we open ourselves up to Him and allow Him to do so.

This is it: my story, your story, our story and now... our *history* — as long as we use the past negative experiences to make positive changes in our lives and in those of other people. My desire now is to make life better for the people that suffered trauma like I did. When we work together — we can have greater impact than walking this tough journey alone! Hence, my exclamation, as this has been the season of discovery. I have been enlightened to a new way of thinking; to see opportunities out of the problems I encountered. So, now I state: *If only I knew then, what I know now!*

Dedication
To those who have ever suffered the horrible, multifaceted spectrums of violence at the hands of trusted loved ones.

To those who have battled; or are going through confusing, emotional, and mental trauma — arising from intimate abusive and toxic relationships or other. That form of suffering has a name —

it is medically called depression; it is an awful enemy, but one can overcome it.

There is a misrepresented, misunderstood, maligned notion about the all-powerful, all-knowing and all-present God; who created us all in love and who longs for a relationship with each one of us. The fact is that He is NOT a harsh God at all.

We read in Genesis 1:27 that God created Adam and Eve as male and female: *"So God created mankind in his own image, in the image of God he created them; male and female he created them."*

God decided to give Adam a suitable helper, so he created Eve out of Adam's rib (Genesis 2:20). It seems like the *helper* is someone who makes the man complete, who is pleasing to him as these verses suggest: *"So, the Lord God caused the man to fall into a deep sleep; and while he was sleeping, he took one of the man's ribs and then closed up the place with flesh. Then the Lord God made a woman from the rib he had taken out of the man, and he brought her to the man. The man said, 'This is now bone of my bones and flesh of my flesh; she shall be called "woman", for she was taken out of man.' That is why a man leaves his father and mother and is united to his wife, and they become one flesh."*
(Genesis 2:21-24, NIVUK).

A woman was created to be useful to a man and so they could work as a team, not a punching bag or to be emotionally bruised. God did not say Eve was to be Adam's slave or to be treated as a second-class citizen or subhuman.

Why do I say this? I was a very disciplined teenager who believed in marriage. I looked after myself for the one person who was going to marry me. Some girls at school would go out with the teachers or date the boys; but not me. My body was the temple of the God. I prayed for God to give me a sign of this man who was to marry me. I wanted it to be the man who will have to ask for my hand in marriage before my parents.

Indeed, the man I had prayed for came to pursue me. He tried everything he could to lure me, to convince me to date him, to have me in his life. He just knew that there was no other way of being with me as I was strict and I stood by my word.

My stubbornness paid off and he finally proposed to me. As soon as I accepted, he rushed to my parents to ask for my hand in marriage. He did the necessary traditional *lobola* rites, including paying the bride price. It was well with me as it showed seriousness and commitment.

The wedding was not one that I had dreamt of. It was a speedy, hurried affair. I did not even choose my dress. I compromised. I was like a whirlwind, rushed, and perhaps if I thought deeply about it — a bit confusing as it was fast-tracked.

I figured it was worth it. He was serious enough to marry me as I had wished. He was prepared to go all out and actually marry me. That spoke volumes to me. Without delay, he straight away took me out of Zimbabwe to the UK because he was English. I was whisked away to a foreign land.

In no time, something went terribly wrong. I could not explain it. I felt the man I married was not the man I that I thought him to be. He was shouting at me and calling me names. He did not want me to go to work or to have friends. I started feeling as though I was a slave. I slogged away. I cleaned, cooked, tried to be a good wife — but it was never good enough, appreciated or considered worthwhile. I managed to push through about going to work; which he did not want me to do. This gave me a peace of mind as I was able to socialise with other people apart from my husband only. That came with serious conditions, I was not allowed to walk to work alone or come back alone.

He would walk me to work and watch me getting in through the gate and the hour I would finish work; he would be by the gate to walk me back home and make sure I did not speak to anyone along the way.

You know, in life people can see a couple walking together holding hands or with one partner's arm around the other — yet the facts are different. Do not be fooled, some of that is done, not in love but controlling the other person. In my case, that was the way of confusing anyone who might want to look more into my life.

My life got tough as I was working in the nursing home, which meant I never finished on time. By the time I was five or 15 mins late, he would be roaring like a lion by the gate — swearing and calling me a prostitute.

He would still walk home with me holding my hand and the shouting would carry on till bedtime. I felt so frustrated, empty, lost because I could not share the traumatic pain which I was going through, with any of my friends; and I had no phone to communication with family — which meant the only chance was through letters. I felt like I was having chains and shackles in the wilderness, alone, yet I mingled with people. His family did not like nor accept me from the very start because they assumed that I would most certainly be a sly gold digger. It was suspicious to them that he had gone to Africa and abruptly returned with such a young timid wife. The only member of his family who accepted me and welcomed me was his twin brother. We got on like a house on fire, we could share jokes and laughter. However, he was an alcoholic, he therefore, had his own insurmountable demons to deal with.

My husband's sister finally accepted me only when she fell sick and I went out of my way to look after her. It is important to overcome evil with good. I showed her just pure love and unconditional care. He did not even go to see his sister or get involved. I believe tit for tat is for the insecure, the immature and the unkind. She then had an opportunity to know me better. She was apologetic of having judged me wrong. Love never fails. She even went to the extent of asking me why I put up with her own brother. My answer was that I married him for better or worse and it definitely got worse for me as he got more mean, nasty, selfish, a self-centred streak.

The name-calling, shouting, swearing and beatings became more and more often. I still believed that with some prayers and being more loving to him would change him. I cooked African cuisine, English dishes and most international meals inspired by my dad who used to be a chef.

The more I did good things for him; the more he told me that I was not good enough. I was bruised internally and externally, inside and outside. I was covered in shame. I was not allowed to go and see friends or make friends. He told me to dress like a Moslem woman, covered from top to bottom even with a burka.

I did not understand why I had to do so. I am Christian. He is not Moslem. No offence to Moslems but I really did not understand that dress code at all; nor appreciate why I had to wear it. It never occurred to me that he wanted me to be invisible. My life turned into a nightmare from which I seemed not to be able to wake up.

I became isolated from my family, friends, or colleagues. He also insisted that we did not plan to return home too soon, for a holiday. I had a smile on my face. But it was fake and plastic. I was not allowed to speak to other people. You see my belief is that marriage is forever. It is not where you just chop and change your mind about who you are with. He became more violent, he would beat me at any given enraged opportunity, drag me by the hair, and throw me against the wall and all sorts of demeaning physical things, threats, and accusation. I could not do anything right. I was not valuable to him or to for that matter, so he told me.

He had charge over all the money in the house and never gave me a penny. He policed and stalked me. I could not get out of his sight. He continued swearing with creative but unprintable and profane words. I would be bombarded with interrogations on why I was late from work, which men had I been talking to and about what. The questions were endless. I would stutter, whimper and stumble as though I was a very naughty child being dragged home from some vile activity.

I remember the one time, when I returned home to Zimbabwe for holidays. He was not expecting me to say anything. He was used to me being a silent, compliant mouse. I took courage in my hands and in the company of my parents I told them of the mistreatment that I endured from him. I also warned them that should I be declared dead, they should not look far. I wanted them to know that he would be the one responsible for murdering me. He just laughed it off and said I was exaggerating and making up stories. He said that he had been joking with me by saying anything like that. Well, he actually did not deny saying it. I remember that my mum worried, and gently taking me aside, she pleaded for me to stay with them. She said it was safe where they were, humble and poor, in Zimbabwe, but it was home to love, with laughter and life. However, she did say that, if I were to choose going back to the UK with my husband, she could not stop me.

She insisted that if things got worse, I was to go to the Zimbabwe Embassy and come back home. This beautiful illiterate soul loved me and gave me a gift of wisdom in my difficult circumstances. We returned to the U.K and, as expected, nothing changed. Rather, the mistreatment escalated.

The final straw came at some point when I remember lying down on the floor covered in cold sweat, looking up at my husband who had turned into a monster. I was silently talking to God, the only God in Whom I have ever believed. I remember saying, "Father, what do I do? What do I say? Why did it come to this?"

I remember the words coming to me from within me clearly saying, "Just say something?"

I repeated, "What, Lord?"

"Just say something?" came back the response.

So, I said to my husband in a very calm voice, "Why are we doing this? We don't need to get to this, do we?"

He then just put the knife down. The minute he placed the knife down, I knew that it was time to do something now or never, for me to run for and with my life. I phoned the police the next day. They were absolutely unhelpful. They said that it was only domestic affair. To them this kind of thing seemed normal. It was a private affair.

Is it not sad that had my husband done the same thing to a woman at the office or in the street, it would be taken seriously? A woman on the street is safer than one who is in her own home. Home, a place of sanctuary, turns into a torture chamber, a prison. We must be careful, when the abnormal is made to seem normal, things become weirder and weirder. I was thinking to myself whether the police wanted me to appear with a knife stuck in my body for them to appreciate that this was a life-threatening situation. I continued calling out for help. I checked abused women from the yellow pages and found a women's group which came to my assistance and evacuation.

I was scared to leave because of the way he was threatening to murder me. I needed help to leave. They came to escort me as I left the house. It was dangerous for me to leave. I had to have security as I was leaving the house. Someone from the shelter came. He threw my clothes in black garbage bags outside on the pavement. I was told to get more things. But I was done. I was sick and tired of being sick and tired of the torture. My little Ford Fiesta and my clothes in disposable rubbish bags was what I had, I fled. I was advised to fight for the house, that I was entitled to half of the house. I was not interested; I was so upset. My heart was so closed up that I wanted absolutely nothing to do with my husband again. I wanted to get as far from him as possible. It had been four-year of torture. Why did I stay so long? I sincerely believed that things would change, that he would see me, love me, appreciate, honour me treat me as precious... one day.

I remember sitting in the shelter, asking God if marriage was good, what was my marriage in that state good for? I heard this very clearly in my mind; God indicating to me that 'this is a Stepping Stone to something'. I had to think about what that meant. I was aware that these were not my own thoughts because the words used were not my usual kind of vocabulary.

As I look back, I realise that I was truly loved by God, I was handpicked for a purpose — taken from my poor family who could never afford an airline ticket to UK. Out of this tragic experience, I managed to find myself because of coming to the UK, I could help my poor family in Africa.

My parents both died young, aged 45 and 56 respectively. Being the oldest child, I became a parent to my six siblings when I was still in my early 20s; helping financially with their education and of their day-to-day expenses.

About four years later, I met another gentleman at a disco with friends. I was now able to go out to dance, to socialise, to have fun, to do down time and leisure. It was so liberating. I was now living life instead of merely existing. I was horrified when I learnt that he shared the same first name with my ex-husband, so I wanted to avoid him at all cost. He was interested in me. It was awkward. My friends then had to explain to him about the name complication. He was patient with me, so that I could get over that weird coincidence. He seemed really nice, kind. He did not appear to have a nasty streak. So, I had to take myself to task. The question this time was: what do I do? How do I proceed? Do

I do it like the last time? Wait for him to marry me? Start life the way I did before? Insist that he marry me first before living with him? I was in a dilemma.

I reasoned that I must date him first and then live with him to get to really know the person that he was. I did not want any more surprises. This time I decided to live with the man before settling for marriage. You can save yourself but be dealt a terrible deck of card. There seems to be no formula, no logbook, to say that you have been good, here is your prize or a good marriage as a reward — or indeed, you deserve a great partner. This guy did not seem like he wanted to live fully with me. We could not make significant plans together; let alone buy a house together. I lived in one room. He seemed not too excited about doing life with me.

He liked us to stay with his parents more. He had a fixed permanent room at his mum's house. It was a small, packed room. You had to squeeze yourself into it. Or he would see me occasionally, only when he felt like it. One bizarre thing was that, while he was a quiet and nice man, a very gentle giant, easy going, with a beautiful calm voice, he never gave me a cent for our upkeep. Not a single penny. He folded his arms but expected to live with me and eat. I struggled to provide. I worked hard. I was unimpressed one day when he had been out to town, but he came back home to tell me that we had run out of coffee and biscuits. I said he should have bought them to replenish, when he went to town. I did not know that coffee and biscuits had run out because I did not consume any of them.

So, here is the scenario — would you believe this: when he did buy them, he wanted reimbursement! I was startled. I did not have the sense to refuse. Neither did I think it necessary to sit down and do a budget and determine who would be responsible for what in our upkeep. He was simply stingy. He appeared more loving than my first husband, he helped me with domestic chores. That seemed loving to me. He did not beat me up, so I thought that was a bonus. One can actually sacrifice themselves, lower own standard so much on the false altar of love! Yet, true love gives generously. He would not do anything with me or for me; that was financially involving. I was clueless that there is such a thing as an economic or financial abuser. He avoided all monetary responsibility, lived with his parents in his late twenties and had no ambition whatsoever, to be independent or leave home. He was not in a hurry to mature.

Since I was in a foreign land with no room of my own, eventually I bought a house for myself. He was not interested. When I got my own house, he decided to move in with me. Even though he was a nice enough man, he was incredibly ungenerous with his money. I kept on in this relationship for another four years. He never gave me a single penny. We had no children. Even in my first marriage I had no fruit of the womb. I longed for a baby. I expressed my need for a child. His response was that infertility had to be my fault, since I had not had a child in my previous marriage. Neither had he... interestingly, up to now he has no child. Well, I suggested that we go for IVF treatment. After investigations, he realised that it would be quite expensive. He opted for a dog, instead. Foolish me, I agreed to getting a pet, as an interim plan though, genuinely believing that when we got enough money, we would do the IVF treatment.

I loved him enough to compromise for a dog. In my view, a dog was fine until we had accumulated enough money for the IVF. The dog was not potty-trained and started pooing and weeing all over the house, my house. I protested; I could not stand it. Not only was my husband more fascinated with the dog than with me. He spent a lot of time with the dog. He spent hours and hours cooing, loving on and fussing over the dog. The dog became the mistress, the third person in my marriage, right there in my house, right in front of my eyes. It was unbelievable. I fed, cleaned up and suffered for that dog. It did not bring me joy but an incredible amount of stress. The smell of dog pooh and urine become the norm. My husband lost interest in me; I did not exist in his world anymore. I would talk to him and he would ignore me. I eventually put my foot down that the dog needed to go, my final straw was when the dog not only urinated on the new sofas but also chewed them. To him it was not an option. He packed his bags, took his dog and he left me.

He walked out of the four-year relationship; just like that with his dog! I was devastated. Had he chosen a dog over me? I felt worthless, useless, hopeless, and helpless — how could this be true? Who can ever say that a dog was a mistress in their relationship? I wept so hard for days till I had no voice, I lost my appetite due to the heartache. I was lost, felt alone, melting away, and becoming ill.

The Bible says in Proverbs 13: 12, *Hope deferred makes the heart sick, but a longing fulfilled is a tree of life." (NIV).* This was my life. When love is not reciprocated, it derails you. I began to lose weight and became a sack of bones. Strangely, in my first relationship I had put on a lot of weight, though I did not cry. I had gained so much weight due to comfort eating, I suppose. Being locked up, jailed and confined — all I could do was work a little and eat a lot. Yet this time, where the man who loved his dog more than me, the opposite happened. I was so aggrieved, unhappy and broken. In my anorexic delirium state, I was saved by a dream. I dreamt that I was in a mental institution. Two attendants kept holding me back, and pushing me to sit down. They dragged me each time I tried to get up and walk. As I looked at the reflection of myself on the window, it appeared like I had very long unkempt dirty locks. I was so skinny. I asked where I was, they said 'you are in Tindal Hospital for mentally ill people' because I had gone mental. They told me I had been there for an extremely long time.

I asked questions about my house; my family; my friends... and my life? All they did with each question was that they would look surprisingly at me. Then afterwards, they would look at each other and shrug their shoulders. They sounded like a broken-down record, saying that it was not their business; they had no clue about what I was asking about, their job was simply to stabilise me. It was scary. I asked them what I was supposed to do to come out of there. They said, "Till you can stand on your own feet, eat and look after yourself." I pleaded with them for food. I needed to eat, to gain strength, to be revived. I had to get out of there. Each time I tried to put food down my throat I would throw up.

I awoke suddenly with tears flowing down my face but relieved that it was just a dream. I had a sense of prompting that I had to pick myself up again, start my life over. I still had questions and was searching for answers. I asked God again what the second relationship was all about. There was silence. In retrospect, I realised that if my second man I met had been generous, we would have bought the house together. His tight-fisted behaviour worked out in my favour for now, as we would have otherwise been entangled in property wrangle.

After a while, one close friend introduced me to another man as I headed for my third relationship! She knew us both and figured that since we had been through trauma, we would be good and kind to each other. I did not know which avenue to use this time around; to get into the relationship. I began to see this man. We clicked and started dating almost straight away. The reasoning kicked in again. We got close and I had let down my guards over the principles I went by before my first marriage. I made different choices in this relationship, no self-preservation.

In the second relationship, I had decided to date and live with the man, with a view to build up with my target of a lifelong marriage. Well, that did not turn out too great. So, for this relationship, I figured out that as soon as I was comfortable, I would be committed and give of myself without holding back, intimately giving myself. I had no idea what to do — except to see how it would go. I decided to go with the flow; taking life on as it came. He invited me over to his place. We would have red wine each time I visited.

Quite romantic; but after daily drinking I began to feel uncomfortable. I don't usually drink that much, so I decided to stop the drinking. He would drink alone — a whole bottle at a time. Then it dawned on me that he had alcohol dependency problems. A serious addiction, this was a professional alcoholic. I had believed that an alcoholic got thoroughly sloshed and would stagger — this one didn't; he was a functional alcoholic!

He was a morning, afternoon, and night drinker. He drank in between working hours. At a party, he was the last man standing when all his other friends were intoxicated. He would be up and walking in a straight line. I also discovered that I instantly fell pregnant. The weirdest thing was that in the previous relationships, I had never fallen pregnant. Not once, therefore I was super excited.

The shock to me was that he was livid. He wanted nothing to do with pregnancy. He told me to terminate the pregnancy, and I was totally against that idea. I could not kill an innocent child. In any case, what if this were to be my only gift of a baby. I decided to keep the pregnancy. Today, this is the only child I have, my delightful daughter. He bailed out and left me at barely 21 weeks pregnant. At full term, when I was in labour... My Care Team called him. I was in distress; I was quite ill. It was a difficult experience of labour into giving birth. He told them that he was not interested, he had moved on to another woman! That was fine by me, I had to hold up.

When she was eight weeks old, I figured I needed to call him to invite him to see his baby. I was alarmed by his cold threat to kill me. "You had better watch over your shoulder. Do you know that I can get you killed? I can get you shot just like that. You can die any moment. You had better watch over your shoulder," he said.

I immediately called the police to inform them that my daughter's father had threatened to kill me. It was at night and they advised me to come to the police station in the morning. The following morning as I stepped out of the house, I was horrified to see petrol literary everywhere at my house. All over the door, the steps, the car, around my house, all the walls were drenched with petrol. He intended to burn us in the house. I have absolutely no clue what stopped him from setting the place alight. What held his hand from striking the match, or drop the cigarette.

There must have been angels of protection dispatched to the house; miraculous protection from God. When I reported it, the police simply said that I was to stay away from him. Surprised at what the police again said in response — I was unsure if this keeping away would do any good — when the person had intruded into my property and planned to cause harm, what was staying away going to do? What if he came for me, again?

That is when darkness began to close in over me. I struggled with this, a double jeopardy for me and the baby as I was no longer on my own. The baby needed me around the clock. I was frightened I had no support besides this added fear. Over time, I decided to seek financial assistance to sustain me with supporting the baby. I had to access social benefits but had made the necessary plans. I kick-started the process of applying for the assistance. I went for the social benefits support; the authorities were not interested in helping me. The response was such that, the system literally spit me out — that is how they rejected me.

I could not pay my bills. There was going to be closure on my house, my very own house. I struggled enormously. Over a period of three years after, life began to turn around for the better for me. A lot happened and I got out the stuffy situation by God's grace.

I now live in a different property and I rent out my house. How all this came about is something that I simply am unable to explain, logically. All I can say is that my God had my back and worked out things for me. Following the three awful relationships, I finally thought that I would be safe on my own. A war began to rage inside me. A storm of frustrations and rejections overwhelmed me. It was confusing. I was fighting an internal battle.

I did not realise that when you have come out of domestic abuse, you are still stuck with very strong negative emotions; bitterness, anger, rage, shame, feeling insecure, unworthy and insignificant! These are real emotions that can be inexplicable for one experiencing them.

Yet another battle churns within you. Abuse mars you, disfigures you internally, imprints a distorted image of your real identity, and lies to you. I realised that I was drowning in anger, shame, and unworthiness. I needed to work through all of those difficult emotions, in a slow but deliberate to a journey of wholeness. I could not move on dragging along unforgiveness, offence, hurt, and the pain with anger that I held against my partners. I had lost myself.

The emotional, physical, financial, mental torment and pain that I had suffered at the hands of my partners held me hostage. I needed to let go of the heavy burden, the negative emotions towards this 'card' that life handed me. On that realisation, I decided to go on a journey, I began to look within, and I sought help; it has been a rewarding process that has brought me here.

Now I am helping women who have been through domestic abuse. I am like a tour guide, not a travel agent. It is not theory that I impart but practicable tools and experience. I have walked the path. I have experienced the torture, the terror, the paralysing from fear. I, however — through God's grace — have overcome. I hope that with this narration of my life journey, though summarised... you are encouraged and strengthened. You too, will overcome.

Lessons Learnt
There is hope in a hopeless world. God's purpose for your existence here on earth is unique, special and specific. None of your experiences — the good, the bad and the ugly —are ever wasted.

From my first husband's access into my life, I saw that he may have been divinely used as a set up for a girl with a poor background. He became a stepping-stone beyond the abuse.

I received the gift of a better socio-economic life in a developed world. He helped in my metamorphosis, from a timid people pleaser and a doormat; to a strong and powerful, useful woman. Whereas I used to be a 'yes' person, because of his behaviour, if something is not sitting right with me, personally and in business... I am able to say 'no'.

From the tight-fisted mean man, who was quite content with his room reserved for him at his mother's home; I learned to provide for myself. I had no room at my parents' home to fall back on, so I worked hard for wealth to become financially independent. From owning my own house, being empowered, and getting transformed. The house which was going to be taken away from me, is one that I now let out as rented property. It is God Who has promoted me, to the extent of becoming a property investor. I now have three properties and looking into acquiring more.

From the father of my child, I got a present. I have lovely and beautiful daughter who has fulfilled me and made my life complete. I was given the priceless privilege and the honour of being a mum.

In the end, all the painful traumatic experiences have moulded me into an effective ambassador for domestic abuse, supporting ladies who have been through the same. Because I truly know how it feels like being on the receiving end of the blows of someone who can turn your life upside down.

The word of God gives assurance that God changes evil into good. **Genesis 50:20-21**, *"'As for you, you meant evil against me, but God meant it for good in order to bring about this present outcome, that many people would be kept alive [as they are this day]. 21 So now, do not be afraid; I will provide for you and support you and your little ones.' So he comforted them [giving them encouragement and hope] and spoke [with kindness] to their heart."* **(AMP)**.

So, now then is the time to think back.

If your sister, mother, friend, partner, betrays you, sells you out, strips you of your coat of many colours, is jealous of you, is wicked, berates and belittles you, schemes against you, know this: in God's divine plan, you are being catapulted to greatness.

How else would Joseph have gone to Egypt as a slave, to eventually end up as the second in command in that nation, if it weren't for God? He was a foreigner; this would not be possible had he not been betrayed and sold by his brothers.

Not once as you read Joseph's story from the pit, to prison, to palace, do you ever see Joseph complain about the wickedness and unfair treatment that he experienced in all those places. At times, other people's opinions do not matter. So, you are not the only one, you are not the first nor the last — to be hurt by someone who you genuinely love.

It is not about you; it never has been about you. Terrible things happen to good people in this cruel world. Many people have gone through the same experiences and others even worse, but God. He is always present, the word of God tells us that He is the same, as He was in the past, so He is at present and will be in the future to come. He is faithful and always loving, thus gives us a wholesome way out of any horrible situation. God is for us and is with us all.

Many Christian women have judged me, as though I do not have a relationship with my God. The fact that I do is what matters. He has always been covering, nurturing protecting me. Some women can see a woman like me getting in and out of relationships and think that it's my fault, that I don't pray enough or something is wrong with me. Some even believes that as a woman it is a shame to the family by walking away from deadly toxic relationships. The same God who put people together can also let us know it is time to walk away from what does no longer serve us.

I pray for his guidance in my work, and for many of my clients — some with whom I may not share the same faith. God is guiding me to help all women that are in devastating situations.

So, are you fighting a battle with your own emotions, finding it hard to let go the pain someone put you through? Anger and bitterness can hold us hostage. There is power in letting go but it is a lesson to learn. I found my true purpose through my pain.

I learned to fight for my life and turned my trauma into transformation. My challenges are my story; this is my testimony of how God loves me because I could have been dead long time ago. You may wonder why I am carrying on talking about God! If it wasn't my belief in God, I truly believe I could have turned out to be alcoholic or become a smoker, drug addict and obese — all this would have been my way of finding a break, to numb the traumatic pain. I have learnt never to judge other people too because God stopped me from the thought of getting easy quick money when I struggled financially with a new born and house bills.

As my name says, I am Glad — and I am truly *glad* and excited to be alive in the season; to be able to help other people with similar challenges to mine — to find their own purpose, to look within and discover who they are. To know that they matter, after feeling worthless and the feeling of not good enough like I did. We are all special and good enough as we are.

If any problems come our way. Let's pick ourselves up dust off and find our true purpose in life. From pain I found my purpose.

8
Righteousness by Faith

STELLA MUROVE

Born Again, Spirit-filled and Speaking in Tongues
THIS is my story as believer. I considered myself to be very strong spiritually, attending church services almost every week, mid-week meetings, conferences as well as all manner of prayer sessions, from individual, to couples, church and all-night prayers. I would engage in individual, family, and corporate church fasts without fail. I was even a leader in my local church for many years. I faithfully participated in, and attended, seminars organised in church. I was a dedicated and devoted member. I was at times able to read and study the word on my own and God, being faithful, would reveal good things that made me enjoy reading the word.

But I was going through the motions. I lacked consistency. My life fluctuated from that of a free believer enjoying the goodness of God to that of a desperate and hopeless Christian who is ignorant of what to do. In those times my heart was characterised by worry. I fretted over anything, really. I was fearful and timid. Anger, guilt, shame, confusion and condemnation leading on to discouragement are part of those attributes I was associated with in those moments. I did not value or honour the word of God in all aspects, really, but I was ignorant of it. For instance, I did not think there was healing for mental sickness or wounds and some other things. In some respects, I did not believe that miracles still happen. I was scared of non-existent things that I created by the imagination in my own heart. At one time, I even enrolled with one Christian organisation, where I had to pay about £500 to be delivered from fear. This eventually did not come to pass as I couldn't afford the money at the time. I ended up enrolling with Charis Bible College as a directive from the Holy Spirit.

The years 2014 and 2015 marked the central part of my story, which is ongoing today. I was an intern then at Charis Bible College Walsall. One of our tutors walked into the classroom and introduced his lesson. As individuals in that class, you were to choose a topic or verse from the Bible to do an in-depth study. After some deliberation on the subject, I gathered that this was not meant to be a topic or subject or verse which was well known to me but rather one I needed to know more about or one I found challenging to my understanding. I remember putting my hand up and asking where we would get the information to study from. John Maunder, the tutor answered, "The Bible is your main source, depending on your relationship with the Holy Spirit. He will reveal to you information and guide you as you study and write the report. Other sources of information could be books on the chosen subject written by Christian authors. He promised to guide us on that area of choosing authors."

We could also use Bible commentaries or interview some Christians on our chosen subject, then report back according to the procedures laid out for the study. To me that sounded a mammoth task, especially when I looked at the time allotted to complete the project.

By the end of that session, after we had prayed, I remember that I chose a verse, "But seek ye first the kingdom of God, and his righteousness; and all these things shall be added unto you" (Mathew 6:33). The whole verse was too big for the task and I had to streamline the study to the topic "Righteousness", which then after all what needed to be done was done this topic was finally changed to "Righteousness by Faith" as the Holy Spirit revealed to me that true righteousness is only received from God by faith in Jesus.

What the Lord Revealed to me about Righteousness

"A picture is worth a thousand words" is an English adage meaning that complex and sometimes multiple ideas can be conveyed by a single still image, which conveys its meaning or essence more effectively than a verbal description by Fred R. Barnard (1921).

It has been said "a picture is worth a thousand words". After college, I got home, ate a small lunch then began my assignment. I asked the Lord to reveal to me what righteousness meant. I had pulled out all scriptures with the words 'righteous' and 'righteousness', and began reading from the Old to the New Testament. They were so many that it proved to me that I was not going to finish and that I needed to start on the work as time was not really on my side. As I was reading and meditating on this concept "Righteousness", I asked the Holy Spirit to reveal to me what righteousness is and what it really means to be righteous in God as a Kingdom child.

The Lord took me in the spirit, stood me right in the centre of my church auditorium. From there, the Lord directed me to look at three very much connected and related pictures, one at a time. I saw a lot going on in the spiritual realm that defines righteousness, of which some of the detail may not be easy for me now to write all on paper.

In the first picture, the Lord showed me the pastor behind the desk, with a Bible in front of him, a note book and a pen. He was in a bubble of his own. It was a beautiful solitary place in which the pastor was studying scriptures and writing down notes. He looked, peaceful, calm, contended and enjoying and loving the word of God in a very peaceful and pure environment. All I know is the pastor was with the Lord, studying the Word of God in a quiet, pure and peaceful environment, enjoying the fellowship as the Holy Spirit was revealing information.

Next, I was to look at the youths, young people who were rehearsing or practising a drama that involved a bit of a sequential dance. Still, I was looking at their "spirit beings" and all was beautiful, peaceful, with full of enjoyment and was the perfect, peaceful environment for them to dance.

With the third picture, I was directed to look at children from about five to 11 years old. They were asking me to teach them dancing. "Teach us to dance," one of them spoke out, looking straight into my eyes and the others nodded in agreement, looking at me as if they were pleading with me. Without even giving it a thought, I found myself teaching them how to dance with demonstrations and instructions. I used the right words to describe how to dance effectively. There was no strain, no stress, no hassle, no confusion; all was smooth going and easy. One of the most difficult things for me to do in my life naturally is to dance and I have never danced that way before. All I knew was I couldn't dance. If I danced, people around me would just laugh because I was not in sync to the tune. But in my spirit, I can dance (Philippians 4:13).

The wisdom I gathered through those three pictures is that one of the characteristic traits in righteousness is purity in every sense; I did not see any sinful deeds, neither did I see any dirt, nor streaks, strands, specks, no impurities of any nature, no taint but just pure clean atmosphere. The scripture that I found linking to this purity is Proverbs 30:4, which says, "Every word of God is pure..." Since God and His word are one, it is very encouraging to know that when God is looking at me, He sees that purity in me. Consequently, when I am looking at my fellow brothers and sisters in the Lord, I see them with the same lens of purity. This helps us to stay united and in good relationships. This also reminds me of a time when I was in my second year in Bible college. I was invited by Yeshuah Ministries' pastor to share a little bit on "Relationships in church". I was looking for what I thought would be a perfect message since I had many of them. But none of them could stick in my heart as a message I was going to share for a short time in a seminar. Just about two days before the conference, The Lord gave me a message titled, *"From now on... we regard no one after the flesh."* **(2 Corinthians 5:16: ESV)**.

I learnt that it was alright to physically separate from others just for the purpose of being with the Lord, talking with the Lord, reading and studying, and meditating on the word of God. In this state, great and mighty things are revealed to you. You receive from God revelations, wisdom, guidance and words of knowledge within a short space of time. This will be for use in your personal life or for your family and also for sharing with others. Pastors, teachers, evangelists and any other sharers of the word get what to share from this state of meeting with just the Lord.

I was reminded of Moses when he went up the mountain to be with the Lord, to receive the Ten Commandments, and came and shared the word of God with the whole congregation (Exodus 32-34). The glory of God reflected from Moses face (Exodus 34:29) when he came down from meeting with the Lord on Mount Sinai with the two tablets of the testimony. I learnt that there is no room for selfishness or meanness in righteousness. What the Lord has passed on to you, freely can be passed onto others. Apostle Paul who went to the desert of Arabia soon after he met with the Lord on the road to Damascus. There he received revelations from God and we read this in nearly two thirds of the New Testament. John, *"...was in the isle of Patmos, for the word of God, and for the testimony of Jesus Christ"* **(Revelations 1:9)**. The Lord revealed to him what he had to write and share with others, *"Blessed is he that readeth, and they that hear the words of this prophecy, and keep those things which are written therein:"* **(Revelations 1:3)**.

Faith is birthed and established in righteousness as you meditate on the Word. Love, joy and temperance are part of righteousness. In righteousness, brothers and sisters respect each other. The younger know how to relate with the older and vice versa. Dancing, drama and playing games is normal. In all the three pictures, there is so much zeal to learn something new, a great willingness to impart knowledge, skills and new things to others from very much knowledgeable people and those with skills at the tip of their fingers. No one is denied any information or knowledge. Unity is in righteousness, so is orderliness—there is no discord, complaints or murmuring, not even envy, jealous or gossip.

In all three pictures peace that surpasses all understanding was outstanding and appeared to me as the medium of operation in righteousness. The atmosphere was peaceful. In righteousness you are at peace with God. Peace is the presence of God. If you removed peace then chaos, confusion, regrets, guilt, shame, fear, condemnation will abound.

What I learnt about righteousness from scriptures and other sources

The dictionary defines righteousness as the state of moral perfection required by God to enter heaven (Expository Dictionary of Bible Words). According to different Bible translations, synonyms of the term righteousness are 'just; right; even; equity, balance' and 'impartial'. Simply put, righteousness being right with God or right standing with God. It is the ability to approach God the father without any sense of unworthiness and condemnation. Kenyon defined righteousness as "the ability to stand in the presence of the father God without the sense of guilt or inferiority. Righteousness comes to us as a free gift in the New Creation, when we are born again. The life and nature of God is "Righteousness".

Anyone who is born again receives the nature of God and automatically becomes the Righteousness of God. My description of righteousness is, "The spirit of Christ in you, that you were baptised in when you received the new life." When God looks at you, He sees His righteous one because He sees His Spirit. When you are in righteousness, this means you have been qualified by God to relate with Him freely without fear or condemnation. This is a perfect relationship in which you receive the peace of God, more so the fruit of the spirit (Galatians 5:22). At the same time, you are translated from the kingdom of darkness into the kingdom of light (Colossians 1:13). You become an heir or a co-heir, together with Christ, of the kingdom of heaven. God becomes your father and Jesus your brother and you become a family member of heaven. Heaven rejoices at this new birth.

Additional Discoveries: Double-Minded

I discovered that, as a born-again Christian, I was living my life and serving the Lord out of the law as well as by the grace of God. I had no clue how I got entangled into the law but now I know that was due to ignorance. In Romance 10, Paul described Jews as zealous for God but not according to knowledge for they were ignorant of the righteousness of God. If you are ignorant of God's righteousness by faith you end up establishing your own righteousness, in which you design your own set of rules, putting Christ aside. Philippians 3:6-9 was an eye opener to me as I read and sought to understand Paul's testimony comparing his life under Judaism/ the law to the life he experienced in Christ Jesus. As regards to righteousness under the law, Paul said he was "blameless".

Righteousness under the law is using self-effort to adhere to what the law commanded. This is worshipping God according to works of the law where you try to please God by doing what the law stipulates. God is already pleased with you in Christ Jesus. It is the opposite of what the **grace of God** offers for righteousness is a gift of God according to 1 Corinthians 5:21. The law was rigorous and numerous as well the scripture says *"...no man is justified by the law in the sight of God."* **(Galatians 5:11)**. And the law is not of faith.

For Paul to testify that he was blameless means he studied and practiced the law according to the book right up to the dot. He called himself "a Pharisee of Pharisees", more erudite among his peers, religious men who were professionals in the law. They knew the law inside out and were able to work under it accordingly. I wasn't as good as that. These men paid tithe of mint and anise and cumin, practicing the law to the maximum. I did not practice the whole law as such. I was not doing it right, for the scripture in **Romans 11:6** says, *"And if by grace, then is it no more of works: otherwise, grace is no more grace. But if it be of works, then it is no more grace: otherwise work is no more work".* This verse tells me that it is either one or the other. There is no way I could mix and expect to get the same results. Either, I serve God under the law or under grace, never under both. *"For as many as are of the works of the law are under the curse: for it is written, Cursed is every one that continueth not in all things which are written in the book of the law to do them."* What it means is I was operating under the curse of the law because I wasn't able to continually do all the things written in the book according to the law. This is very serious. I tell you the truth that I would fast according to the law expecting God to answer my prayers and grant my requests because I fasted 40 days or three days or five days. Now I know that "Christ has redeemed us from the curse of the law…" so I am not cursed and I have chosen the grace of God because I now know the truth.

I had a "need" and asked for prayer from colleagues and one of them told me that the Lord revealed to her that my problem was not the need but my belief system. She said I was fluctuating; at one time I was in the sunshine believing God and at another time I was in the gloomy period of doubting. She said that I needed to just believe and not doubt, for a double-minded person gets nothing from the Lord (James 1:6–8). A double mind is having in the mind opposing views at different times, being inconsistent and unstable in your ways and convictions. That's exactly how I was, not putting my trust in the Lord all the way. I was at times taking matters in my hand, through worry, trying to sort things on my own so that they come out the way I wanted them to be. And yet the Bible says, "…The just shall live by faith".

***

Peace versus worry/doubt/fear/discouragement/ confusion/ condemnation
The world's idea of peace is absence of problems, difficulties, trials and tribulations. Jesus promised that in the world we will have problems but he encouraged us that we should be of good cheer because he has overcome the world. It is not the absence of difficult situations that brings peace in our lives. Falling apart like a two-dollar suitcase is a symptom of lack of peace so is running about like a headless chicken. Fear, confusion, worry, discouragement, doubt and condemnation are all symptoms of lack

of peace. Sickness, lack, accidents, death, drought, hurricanes, storms, tsunamis, divorce and others alike, are all potential sources of lack of peace. All these cited things do not come from God. Jesus promised, *"Peace I leave with you, My peace I give to you; not as the world gives do I give to you. Let not your heart be troubled, neither let it be afraid"* **(John 14:27)**.

Peace, from a godly perspective, is the presence of God. Peace is not dependent on circumstances around you. Rather in the midst of those circumstances we are to let God manifest his peace. Peace is defined as at one again or just one or joined. Peace originates from being at one with God, then living in agreement with God, as we are together with the Lord. If I am at peace with God, this then empowers me to be at one with myself spirit soul and body. In this state God will be in a position to manifest peace in any situation of my life because I am operating from a position of power, the power of peace will be evident and will permeate around me.

One day I was driving to work, talking with the Lord and asking for peace in my workplace. The Lord responded immediately with a question: "Where is peace?" I answered, "In my heart." That settled the matter. I just burst into praise and worship because I understood that the Lord was saying I should just draw peace from the well of righteousness inside of me. I just needed to realise that wherever I am that is where peace is. I am not without peace at any moment and at any place. And yet the previous day, I had exchanged words in a heated argument with one of the seniors at work pertaining to my work conditions (I didn't know she was a senior; she had to tell me behind closed doors, and I apologised) but I was involved, rather at the centre of the row. The whole scenario left me feeling not so good as it seemed unavoidable. I wished I had a way of doing it differently but it happened that way. Thank God that incident helped trigger change for the better for the organisation.

At some time, I was staying with a friend, Monica. She told me all she wanted in life was peace. There is torment in the absence of peace. I asked her to explain what she meant. Monica added that she wanted some quietness and rest in the house. Monica was right as quietness and rest define peace but Monica did not know how to get that in her house especially living with her emotionally disturbed husband Jim. Monica thought if Jim could control his temper and live quietly, then peace would come in the house. I explained to Monica that was temporal but the lasting true peace comes from union with God. This kind will stay on and no one can take it away from you unless you neglect it yourself or give it away yourself. Monica did not seem to agree with me so we left it at that point saying we would revisit the subject sometime later. However, Monica allowed me to pray with her as I spoke peace into her heart. I told her that she could find the peace of God in the midst of any chaos or storm of life just by believing and trusting in God. No one is exempt from going through life storms. Peace is of the heart, and without the peace of God you will respond to life with fear.

Jim, on the other hand, began to apologise to both me and Monica whenever he erupted in uncontrolled temper situations. One day he confessed that he didn't know how to help the situation. But at the same time, he didn't want to hear about "this God" thing he calls it.

Peace is the medium of operation in righteousness. There is no room for worry. *"Thou wilt keep him in peace, whose mind is stayed on thee: ..."* **(Isaiah 26:3)**. This verse is saying the Lord will keep you in peace if you stay focused on him. The question is how do I keep my mind on him? My answer is: re place that worry, that negative thinking which stops you from falling asleep, straight away with the word of God. Get one scripture, think about that scripture. You can use scripture of the day that is posted onto your phone if you downloaded the Bible up. Or these days so many ministers post messages on the media. Read at least one message. I guarantee you that there will be at least a reference to a scripture if they are Bible- believing ministers. Take a scripture, probably one that stands out to you or is highlighted to you by the Holy Spirit. Meditate on that scripture by going over it several times asking the Holy Spirit to reveal what it means, jot down any thoughts you have about that scripture.

Meditating on the scripture helped me stop worrying particularly when I'm going to bed, especially if I'm sleeping in a new environment, be it a hotel or I have visited some friends and relatives. For me, it was as soon as I put my head on the pillow, instead of falling asleep like what others would do I reflect on the day activities, analysing them or begin to think about several issues be it about family, personal, how I interacted with so and so during the day, how they responded or how I reacted, or it could be about bills, finances, food, what to cook, or what to eat. The scripture says do not worry about such things (Matthew 6:33). To someone who has been living a life of worrying, this might take a good resistance by just getting a scripture and meditate on it instead of waiting to be bombarded by several thoughts in which you end up succumbing to. **Philippians 4:8** say "...Think on these things," thus meditate on what is true, honest, just, pure, lovely, good report, virtuous, praise worthy.

About 20 years ago, a friend of mine, Lucy, invited me to a ladies' conference at Rest Haven in Zimbabwe for three days and three nights. She paid for everything, including food and accommodation, even though most of the delegates were fasting. The conference was held during school holidays and as a school teacher, I had no excuse not to go. I thought it was a good time to wind off for both my friend and I. On Thursday morning, in the first official prayer meeting for the conference, we went into the auditorium and, by a quick scan, I noticed that everyone, except Lucy and I, was dressed in either a blue rob or white long dress.

I began to wonder what was happening and who those ladies were and where they were coming from. All that could have been explained to me before but I did not expect them to be dressed like that. In my pre-conceived idea and from some stories I had heard, I thought I was cheated to join and worship with a cult. I don't remember if the word was read but what I remember is that everyone was praying seriously and seemed connected with what they were doing except for me who was looking around and wondering what the next move would be. I couldn't ask Lucy because she was deep in prayer and wouldn't want to disturb her. I couldn't leave the meeting because I didn't know where else to go. Rest Haven is in the middle of a forest and mountains. I was also gripped by fear of the unknown. Instead, I handed over the situation to God. With my eyes closed, I told God that I was scared, I don't know these people, I felt cheated to come, only because I wanted to spend a weekend in Rest Haven, a place I just like to be. I said, "Lord help me because I don't know what to do. I am worried." In response, the Lord opened up heaven in front of me.

A transparent sliding double door automatically opened sideways for me to enter. I stepped in with contentment and joy but well-composed. Immediately, the Lord joined me. We were just taking a walk in a peaceful and quiet environment in this beautiful golden street. The plants on the roadsides were full of life. The temperature was just right. The environment was clean and clear in our father's Kingdom. We walked for a distance such that I could not see where we had started from. We got to a T-junction and my companion said, "Let's turn to the left."

Then, I said, "NO!"

All I can say for now is that I saw the beauty of nature in a very peaceful environment. That peace was beyond my understanding. I cannot even describe it on paper.

Peace is the outstanding character trait in heaven and the Kingdom (Romans 14:17). My husband and I had this scripture inscribed on our wedding invitation cards. We both had experienced the peace of God even in the difficult situations of life. And we did this as a reminder to ourselves that the peace of God trumps over any situation in our marriage right from start. The peace of God that surpasses all understanding is our inheritance in righteousness (Phil 4:7).

Worry, confusion, discouragement, condemnation and guilt etc. cannot stand a chance in the presence of God's. They are totally destroyed and we can live at peace. First experience peace with God by giving your life to Christ. If you are a born-again Christian, then you should know that you are in right-standing with God. Secondly, be at peace with yourself and then with others. Prayer helps get rid of any negative thoughts that come around. Take a moment to cast your cares unto Jesus and not unto friends and other people. *"... in everything by prayer and supplication with thanksgiving let your requests be made known unto God"* **(Philippians 4:5)**. And the peace of God will guard your hearts and minds against fear, worry, condemnation and discouragement.

"The chastisement for our peace was upon Him!" **(Isaiah 53:5)**. Jesus died for our peace. His death provided for our peace, just as it provided for the forgiveness of our sins and healing of our bodies. Knowing that we are in right standing with God gives us the security to remain in peace. Peace was provided for on the cross. Being ignorant of this truth will get us crippled with fear, worry or anxiety and these are not part of righteousness. We should not allow any provision of the cross to go unfulfilled and unappropriated in our lives.

"In righteousness shalt thou be established: thou shalt be far from oppression; for thou shalt not fear: and from terror; for it shall not come near thee" **(Isaiah 54:14).** Perfect love casts out fear and this means that I know that I'm loved and God gives me the grace to remain in peace.

SALVATION PRAYER

Lord Jesus thank you for humbling yourself and coming on earth to save us. Forgive me for living my life the way I desire and not acknowledging you. I have seen that you are Lord and I answer the call of salvation by inviting you to come into my heart. I acknowledge that you died on the cross and shed your blood to set me free. I acknowledge that you rose again and are alive sitting on the right-hand side of the Father. Forgive me for making myself lord of my life and living a life I desire to live without your involvement. Wash me clean, purify and cleanse me and adopt me in the family of God. Fill me with grace to follow and obey you as well as live a life pleasing to you. Pour the Holy Spirit in me and baptise me with fire with evidence of speaking in tongues. I am yours and you are mine now, I declare that I belongs to you God. Thank you for I will now live-in eternity with you.

AMEN.

The Risen Lady Series
The Risen Lady series is an ongoing compilation of short stories with different seasonal titles.
Contact "The Risen Lady" on social media to feature in one of their publications.

Risen Ladies Ministry
Alongside "The Risen Lady" book series is Risen Ladies Ministry, A ministry that empowers the woman to rise to her true potential. To whom she has been created to be in life by breaking through life's trials, bondages, and hardships. The ministry is worldwide and is under the umbrella of *Loveflow Ministries Global*. It engages in weekly prayer, annual conferences, retreats and workshops.

Printed in Great Britain
by Amazon